PRAISE FOR *PROVOCATIVE GOD*

Dr. Dan Lacich is one of the most engaging biblical thinkers I know. He does not just perfect our understanding of Scripture, but draws us closer to Christ and gives us the practical insights we need to walk out that relationship in our everyday life. Written with wonderful illustrations and practical insights, this book will be the tool you were looking for to dig deeper into Scripture and to know more personally God's guidance for your life.

DR. JOEL C. HUNTER, SENIOR PASTOR
NORTHLAND - A CHURCH DISTRIBUTED

I consistently find Lacich an extraordinarily insightful commentator and guide—at once impassioned and on-target about life—a very valuable thinker.

MARCIA PALLY, AUTHOR
THE NEW EVANGELICALS
TEACHES AT NEW YORK UNIVERSITY.

Dan has been my pastor, mentor and friend. When he speaks, I listen. His words in this book aren't just provocative but also life-giving.

BRIAN TOME, FOUNDING PASTOR
CROSSROADS CHURCH, CINCINNATI, OHIO

Dan Lacich is a rare mixture of knowledge and zeal. He eats, sleeps and lives evangelism/discipleship. He is a practitioner, a man who is willing to get his hands dirty. At the same time, Dan knows what he believes and why he believes it. I have no doubt this book will be an inspiration to all who take the time to read it. But be prepared to do more than just read. You will be pressed to action!

DR. DAVID NELMS PRESIDENT AND FOUNDER
THE TIMOTHY INITIATIVE

Provocative God is an incredible reminder of our considerable God, who is also generous and compassionate. Dan Lacich is a gifted storyteller and experienced theologian. Embracing a realistic understanding of the God of the Bible is the best thing that we can do as Christians.

KEN EASTBURN, DIRECTOR OF HOUSE2HOUSE MINISTRIES
AND AUTHOR OF *U R THE CHURCH*.

1

As a child, I heard, "You just have to have faith," whenever I asked an adult a challenging question about the nature of God. So I stopped trying to engage with God in the first decade of my life. Dan Lacich challenges us to think about and to engage with God differently. He offers a relationship with a God who wants us to use the brains He gave us, to ask hard questions, to demand proof so that we may be more effective ambassadors for Him. What you read in this book may, at times, annoy you, make you smile or challenge you—all signs that you are deepening your relationship with our provocative God.

ANN ZUCCARDY, SPEAKER/AUTHOR
AZ COMMUNICATIONS, LLC, HUNTINGTON, VERMONT

We serve a mighty God, and Dr. Dan Lacich is reminding us very clearly of that fact. Our God is, indeed, provocative. We do not take that matter seriously in the world today. Dr. Lacich is an excellent Bible teacher and brings that teaching to life in his new book by forcing us to consider Scripture in a fresh way. Dr. Lacich gets to the heart of the matter in *Provocative God.* You will encounter many new insights that will open your eyes and widen your perspective of our God.

BILL TILLMANN, DIRECTOR OF ADVANCEMENT
ASBURY THEOLOGICAL SEMINARY, ORLANDO, FLORIDA

For many people Christianity creates a comfort zone, like a kind of insurance policy. I'm covered against sin, I've got my ticket to heaven. Dan Lacich shows in his book that the God of the Bible can be extremely provocative. Journeying with this God is a thrilling adventure, full of surprises and excitement, even painful sometimes—but never dull and boring. *The Provocative God* is a challenging map that will benefit every follower of Jesus on their journey with the living God.

DR. LEON OOSTHUIZEN
VREDELUST CHURCH, CAPE TOWN SOUTH AFRICA

God is on the move, and yet much of His church seems to be sleeping. Dan provokes Christians to wake up and assert their God-given, exciting mantle in advancing His amazing Kingdom. My prayer is that God uses this book to awaken His church to the extraordinary works He calls us to walk in. He gets the glory, and we get abundant joy and reward!

DAN HITZHUSEN, INTERNATIONAL VP
E3 PARTNERS

THE

RADICAL THINGS GOD HAS SAID AND DONE

PROVOCATIVE

DR. DAN LACICH

GOD

KUDU

The Provocative God: Radical Things God Has Said and Done
by Dr. Dan Lacich

Copyright © 2014 by Dr. Dan Lacich
Cover design by Dede Caruso
Back cover photo by Stephen Thomas

Published by Kudu Publishing

Print ISBN: 9781938624919
eBook ISBN: 9781938624926

The Provocative God is also available on Amazon Kindle, Barnes & Noble Nook and Apple iBooks.

CONTENTS

ACKNOWLEDGMENTS

NY TIME A PROJECT LIKE THIS IS undertaken and completed there are more people to thank and recognize than one can imagine. That is certainly the case with *Provocative God*. Such support has come not only in the form of direct help with the project but also includes the countless ways people have shaped not only my thinking but also my relationship with Christ and growth as a person. With that in mind I give special thanks to:

Holly Travis Cameron whose faith in and love of the Lord first introduced me to the provocative person of Jesus Christ.

Brian Tome who first insisted that I needed to write for publication if I intended to use the gifts God has given me.

Dwight and Debbie Johnson for their life-long friendship and provision of a little slice of heaven in north Georgia making it possible to finish the book. See you soon Dwight.

My early mentors, Scott Jones, Terry Stoops, Howard Perdue, and Lynn Edwards. I learned the foundations of following Christ and making disciples in your presence.

The staff and congregation of Northland Church; Pastors Joel Hunter, Gus Davies, Kevin Urichko, and Vernon Rainwater who so often provide insights into God that I find encouraging and challenging. Rob Andrescik for his vast knowledge of writing and publishing that guided me so well and encouraged this project. The 9:00 AM Bible class that so patiently endures my rabbit trails. Marc McMurrin, Sean Cooper, Jeff Bell, Jeremy Jobson, Robert Johnson and Peter Geiger for their fellowship and discussions of all things ministry and life. Dede Caruso for her provocative cover art and bookmark design.

Eva Loosier, Sean Bates, Douglas Fielder, Tim Brown, Liz Gritter, Kris Siegmundt, Joseph Eric Jones, David Stupay, Jan Brooks, Tamara Wetterman, Maureen and Stephen Cleary, Cathy Ma, Dusty Cooper, Jim and Rachel Lander, Jon and Debra Kolb, Tom and Melinda Jarzynka and Zach Young for their significant support of the publication of this book.

The gifted team at Kudu Publishing, especially Matt Green and Martijn van Tilborgh, for their faith in the project and willingness to risk what it took to get it published.

DEDICATED TO

The Father, Son and Spirit.
What is more provocative than One God in Three Persons?

Barbara Maguire Lacich, the love of my life MTYLTT

Zachariah, Justin and Garrett, my pride and joy

Special thanks to Larry Carney, Barb McCay and Kandi
Gwynn for support above and beyond

INTRODUCTION

"In the year that King Uzziah died I saw the Lord sitting upon a throne, high and lifted up; and the train of his robe filled the temple. Above him stood the seraphim. Each had six wings: with two he covered his face, and with two he covered his feet, and with two he flew. And one called to another and said:

'Holy, holy, holy is the Lord of hosts;
the whole earth is full of his glory!'

And the foundations of the thresholds shook at the voice of him who called, and the house was filled with smoke. And I said: 'Woe is me! For I am lost; for I am a man of unclean lips, and I dwell in the midst of a people of unclean lips; for my eyes have seen the King, the Lord of hosts!' " —Isaiah 6:1-5

WHATEVER HAPPENED TO a God who was bigger than our wildest imaginations, more grand than our greatest accomplishments, more perplexing than our deepest scientific theories? Whatever happened to the God before whom Isaiah trembled, certain that he would literally be undone by the very presence of such overwhelming holiness and majesty? Whatever happened to that God of mystery, of power, the God before whom we were compelled to fall on our faces and declare, "I am ruined"?

Nearly sixty years ago, J.B. Phillips wrote a book called *Your God Is Too Small.* It was an attempt to stem the growing tide that viewed God as a being we could fully understand and with whom we could be totally at ease. In essence, it was an attempt to keep us from putting God in a box that we could control and open and close at our own discretion. Phillips wanted people to understand that God was far more than the comfortable caricature that many had made Him to be. Certainly He is a

God in whom we find comfort and peace. But He is also a God who at times challenges us, befuddles us, and provokes us out of our comfort zone into a wild and wondrous relationship with Him. Sadly, from the look of things, Phillips failed badly. For many people, Christian and non-Christian alike, God has become even smaller, more manageable, subject to our ever-changing and shrinking notion of what He is like and what He can and even should do.

What is desperately needed is a God who is anything but tame and controllable. We need a God who shakes us out of our malaise. We need a God who provokes us. We need a provocative God. In our highly sexualized culture the word "provocative" normally brings up images of the window at Victoria's Secret, or worse. For something to be provocative it simply needs to get a reaction out of us. You can certainly be provoked sexually. But you can also be provoked into action because of the injustice of human trafficking. You can be provoked to anger like Jesus was when confronted with the thievery that was taking place in the Temple in the name of God (Luke 19:46). You can also be provoked into breathtaking wonder when standing at the pinnacle of Colorado's Pikes Peak, gazing out over the snow-capped mountains around. You can be provoked into a state of confusion and bewilderment when your preconceived notions are smacked in the face by overwhelming evidence to the contrary.

If we really understood God we would know that He is nothing if not provocative. God says and does things that should get some kind of reaction out of us. The very fact that God declares, "For my thoughts are not your thoughts, neither are your ways my ways, declares the Lord" (Isaiah 55:8), should tell us that our encounters with Him should be provocative. They should provoke us to think and live in ways we have never before considered—or, if we have considered them, we too easily discarded them as unreasonable, uncomfortable, or unnecessary.

When we look closely at the Bible, not simply skimming through or looking only for the proof text that makes us feel better, we are confronted by a God who said and did some rather radical, extraordinary, strange, disturbing, and at times frightening things. They are things that challenge us and make us uncomfortable and at times confused. They are things that we often ignore because we don't want to face the implications of what God has said or done. But face them we must if we are ever going to have the kind of relationship with Him that God intends. We need to face them because those who would oppose God point to these provocative statements and actions and twist them into accusations against God.

It is my hope that what you are about to read provokes you. Sometimes it will cause you to wonder at your view of God and hopefully cause you to reconsider and maybe even discard the box you have Him in. Sometimes it will cause you to repent of attitudes and actions. Sometimes it will cause you to have a better understanding of what God expects of you. I know I have had all those reactions and more. Certainly there will be things you read that you disagree with, maybe even passionately. I'm okay with that. In fact I am more than okay with it. I welcome it. Because that means you are engaging with God on a head and heart level that will result in God being bigger in your life than He was before and your relationship with Him being deeper than ever.

REDEFINING "RADICAL"

The subtitle to this book about our provocative God is *Radical Things He Has Said and Done.* The word "radical" has been thrown around a lot lately. David Platt has written a very popular book by that title. The media refers to radical fundamentalists of various religious stripes. On the political scene the far Left and Right are viewed as unreasonable radicals who are threatening the democratic process. And when we think about radical things that God has said and done, our first thoughts most likely concern things that are far out on the extreme, unreasonable, on the edge of rationality if not over it. That is not the understanding of radical that this book presents.

Let's take a look at some dictionary definitions of "radical":

rad·i·cal [rad-i-kuhl] adjective

1. *of or going to the root or origin; fundamental: a radical difference.*

2. *thoroughgoing or extreme, especially as regards change from accepted or traditional forms: a radical change in the policy of a company.*

3. *favoring drastic political, economic, or social reforms: radical ideas; radical and anarchistic ideologues.*

4. *forming a basis or foundation.*

5. *existing inherently in a thing or person: radical defects of character.*

Of the five definitions given at *Dictionary.Reference.com* for "radical" as an adjective, only numbers two and three fit the common usage previously mentioned. Numbers one, four, and five collectively define what I mean by radical. Something that is radical is something that goes to the root or core. It should come as no surprise, then, that we get the English word "radish" from the root word for radical. No pun intended, but it makes the point. Something that is radical should be something that is at the root, heart, core, and foundation of who and what we are.

In speaking of a radical God, what we are really talking about are things that God has said and done that should be at the root of who we are and what we believe. They are things that, as definition five says, are "foundational" to who God is. If they seem radical by our common usage, meaning extremist, then it is not because these things are on the edge and we are at the core. Rather, the radical things God has said and done seem extreme because we have moved far from the root and core of who God is and who He has made us to be. We are the ones who, in our modern and post-modern world, have moved far from the root. We have moved far from the core of where we were created to be. We have drifted ever so slowly to the extreme edges. It is like my friend Pete Geiger sings in his song, "Hallowed Ground": "We've wandered so far off track we didn't know that we were lost." God is still at the center. We are on the edge. We have wandered far off course in our thinking and our actions.

God seems extreme in so many ways because our self-centered perspective has the world revolving around us. We all see ourselves as average, middle of the road, stable, and reasonable. When God does things and says things that are consistent with His character, when He is radical in the foundational sense, He seems extreme and outlandish to us. We grow uncomfortable with this extreme, radical God. So we marginalize and ignore Him and become functional agnostics. Some of us become angry atheists who cry out against a God we don't even believe exists. Some of us turn our back on our radical God and remake Him in our own image; He is safer that way. We can control and understand such a god. But such a god is no God at all. Such a god is a tame, manageable, cosmic security blanket who never meddles in our personal affairs and never challenges our self-centered thinking. To paraphrase C.S. Lewis, such a god is "safe, but not good." We need a God like Aslan, who Lewis describes as "good but not safe." We need a God who will pull us back to the root, the core, the center of who we are made to be.

The God of the Bible is much like the majestic Aslan from The Chronicles of Narnia, who is strong, powerful, and demanding, yet gracious, sacrificial, and merciful. Instead we have a God who is like the lion from the movie, *Secondhand Lions*. He looks like a lion and seems powerful and frightening, initially provoking fear, only to be revealed as an old, worn-out, tamed lion who just wants to lie in the shade and eat dried lion food from a bag.

15

Make no mistake. In the Bible there are lots of very uncomfortable things that God has said and done. Asking you to forgive someone seventy times seven when they sin against you is extremely provocative. Requiring you to love your enemy, the person next door who constantly blares their music at all the wrong times, shoots off fireworks till well past midnight on every conceivable holiday, and lets their trash blow into your yard, is radical and provocative. Saying that the only way to get to heaven is through a relationship of faith and trust in Jesus Christ is as countercultural as you can get these days, and provocative in the extreme. With these and many other things that God has said and done, we have softened them, reinterpreted them, explained them away, and outright ignored them. In doing so we have attempted to tame our provocative God. But He refuses to be tamed. His Word stands for all time and continually calls us back into a relationship with Him that is unsafe, and uncomfortable—but is good beyond our wildest dreams.

SECTION ONE:
YOUR RELATIONSHIP WITH GOD

CHAPTER 1

I SEE "GOD" PEOPLE

"Then God said, 'Let us make man in our image, after our likeness. And let them have dominion over the fish of the sea and over the birds of the heavens and over the livestock and over all the earth and over every creeping thing that creeps on the earth.' " — Genesis 1:26

" 'The God who made the world and everything in it, being Lord of heaven and earth, does not live in temples made by man, nor is he served by human hands, as though he needed anything, since he himself gives to all mankind life and breath and everything.' " — Acts 17:24-25

"Why was the human race created? Or at least why wasn't something creditable created in place of it? God had His opportunity. He could have made a reputation. But no, He must commit this grotesque folly—a lark which must have cost Him a regret or two when He came to think it over and observe effects." — Mark Twain

I N THE 1999 MOVIE, *The Sixth Sense,* we heard that chilling line from adorable little Haley Joel Osment, "I see dead people." This little boy was blessed—or cursed, depending on your perspective—with the ability to see dead people walking about. They were dead people who had not moved on from this world. In the case of the main character, played by Bruce Willis, he didn't even know he was dead yet. Osment's character saw him and knew he was dead. He recognized something about Willis that Willis didn't recognize about himself.

19

When you look at other people what do you see? When you look at yourself in the mirror or look at the actions of your life, what do you see? Better yet, what does God see? For many of us it is uncomfortable and a bit frightening to consider what it is that God sees when He looks into our hearts and lives. When God looks at you does He see something in you that you don't see? Does He see something that pleases Him and makes Him smile? The answer is a resounding yes! When God looks at you He sees something that very few people can see. He sees Himself. He sees God people. God has made you, in some fashion, as an image of Himself. When He sees you there is a very real sense in which God sees His image, His character, and His representative to the world.

The recognition that God sees something of Himself in you and that He put it there should naturally cause a certain amount of amazement and wonder. It should result in an overwhelming sense of being valuable and important. But before you get too far ahead of yourself with that thought keep this in mind: God doesn't need you. In spite of all that you may have heard about how special and valuable you are, in spite of all the efforts to boost our collective self-esteem as human beings, we must come to grips with the fact that God doesn't need us. He doesn't need me and He doesn't need you. God could have continued on throughout all eternity and never missed us in the least. He could have existed quite nicely without us. He could have created everything involved in the first six days of creation, all the way up to the most amazing of animals, and left us out. The world and God—Father, Son, and Spirit—would have gone on rather nicely without us. God certainly could have stopped creating before He ever got around to forming Adam and breathing life into him. Creation of the universe did not require that people inhabit it. Creation doesn't need us and neither does God. Creation would have been just fine without us mucking it up. The Apostle Paul made it clear that God doesn't need us when, as recorded in Acts 17, he preached to the Greeks in Athens and said as much:

"The God who made the world and everything in it, being Lord of heaven and earth, does not live in temples made by man, nor is he served by human hands, as though he needed anything, since he himself gives to all mankind life and breath and everything" (Acts 17:24-25).

He is complete without us. He doesn't need us to build Him a Temple. He doesn't need us to serve Him. Rather the opposite: we desperately need Him.

The case could be made that we human beings are useless, unnecessary, and even detrimental to creation. That may come as a shock to you, especially in light of a culture that seeks at every turn to affirm how special you are, how unique and valuable to the world you are, and even that God might not be able to get on very well without you. Even within the evangelical world it is not unusual to hear a sermon telling you that you are so special to God that if you were the only person on Earth, Jesus would still have gone to the cross for you. I have no intent to try to downplay the love that God has for His creation or the willingness of the Father and the Son to endure the cross, even if just for you. I would never downplay the cross, if for no other reason than that the cross of Calvary is about as provocative as God gets. Yet what concerns me about the "Jesus would have gone to the cross just for you" preaching is that it is built on speculation since the Bible never speaks to that, as far as I know, and it can reinforce a sense of special entitlement that is built on current cultural ideas and not the biblical reason we are special to God. But the bottom line is that God did not need to create us, yet for His own reasons and purposes He did. That should provoke a reaction from us. We should at the very least wonder why God made us.

THE SELF-SUFFICIENT GOD

Classic theology speaks of God's attributes. What we mean by the term "attributes" is the various powers, personality traits, and qualities that make God the being that He is. Most people have some understanding of the classic attributes of God being omnipotence, omnipresence, and omniscience, meaning God is all-powerful, always present, and all-knowing. Yet there is so much more to God. He is love (1 John 4:16). He is three times holy (Isaiah 6:3). He is a jealous God (Exodus 20:5). God is righteous and just (Deuteronomy 32:4). The list goes on and on.

Of all the many attributes of God, one that gets little or no attention is the one that concerns us now. It's the independence of God. He is totally self-sufficient. He is lacking nothing and needs nothing, not from us or from anything. Think of it this way, if God needed something outside Himself in order to be God, then He would be subject to and dependent on that thing or being. It would have some control over God and would supplant God in some way. If God needed something or someone else to cause Him to exist, then that thing, being, or cause would be God. God is dependent on nothing and no one else. God is self-existent. He needs nothing else in order to be. Theologians call this attribute, "aseity." It is such a rare word that spellcheck has never heard of it! It comes from two Latin words that mean "from self" or "of oneself." God exists and has always existed as Father, Son, and Spirit, a perfect relationship of harmony, love, and unity "from Himself" or "of Himself."

Yet for some reason, in spite of His aseity, his self-sufficiency, God made a decision that changed nearly everything. God chose to create, to make the heavens and earth and all that is in them. He made a multitude of plants and animals whose variety is stunning. Finally, He decided to add the crowning jewel to that creation. He decided to make you and me and every other human being who ever walked the earth. In light of God's aseity and self-sufficiency we need to ask ourselves a very important question. Why in the world did God create humanity?

Some, Mark Twain among them, have wondered, given our predilection to sin, if maybe God and creation wouldn't have been better off without us human beings. Twain calls the creation of humanity "this grotesque folly." He is convinced that God must have experienced deep regret over the creation of human beings. Twain seems to think that the creation of humanity was some spur-of-the-moment idea that God never really thought through. Once He made us humans, He must certainly have wished that He had stopped with the lion or the buffalo or any of the other more majestic beasts. After all, we seem to have messed up things royally, starting with the fall of Adam and Eve and leading all the way up through the wars, violence, slavery, greed, and brutality that current headlines remind us of each day.

All of that death and carnage can be directly traced to sin and that takes us back to Genesis 3 and the story of Adam and Eve, a garden, and a serpent. Without going into all the possible theological debates on this passage, there is one thing that is abundantly clear. God had placed Adam and Eve in a creation that was free from pain and suffering, free from broken relationships, free from sin, free from guilt, and free from shame. But the decision of our ancestors to reach for and grasp at equality with God brought a curse on the land and put separation from God at the core of being human. It also meant that death now became the enemy we could never defeat.

But it wasn't always like that. When God put Adam and Eve in the garden of Eden, when He created them, and ultimately us, it was with a far different outcome in mind. God created the galaxies, placed the stars in their courses, gave majesty to the heavens and glory to the mountains. He made the birds to fly, fish to swim, and all the myriads of other creatures doing what they do for His own glory and pleasure. Then He topped it off with humanity made in His image. He topped it off with making a people whose ultimate purpose was finding their ultimate delight in Him, thus bringing Him even greater glory. We were made by God in order to bring even greater glory to Him. We were made to be in a relationship with God that is first and foremost one of worship.

As Jesus approached Jerusalem on what has become known as Palm Sunday, the crowds cheered, danced, and sang His praise. The uptight religious leaders were offended by such an outpouring of praise being heaped upon Jesus. The told Him to make the people stop glorifying him. His response was stunning: *"I tell you, if these were silent, the very stones would cry out"* (Luke 19:40).

Jesus was saying that creation itself was bursting at the opportunity to give praise to God who had come in the flesh. If humanity, ultimately created for that purpose, would not do so, then the rocks and trees would surely burst into praise.

There are numerous places in the Bible that point to the role creation has in glorifying God:

"The heavens declare the glory of God, and the sky above proclaims his handiwork" (Psalm 19:1).

"The mountains melt like wax before the Lord, before the Lord of all the earth. The heavens proclaim his righteousness, and all the peoples see his glory" (Psalm 97:5-6).

"And one called to another and said: 'Holy, holy, holy is the Lord of hosts; the whole earth is full of his glory!'" (Isaiah 6:3).

So we too are made to give praise and glory to God. But just what does that mean and how did God intend for it to happen? For that we need to understand what it means to be made in the Image of God.

HUMANITY: THE CROWNING JEWEL OF CREATION

For all our progress as human beings, all the advancements in technology, medicine, and social science, we seem to have lost ground in a most important area. We have lost our sense of dignity. In fact we seem to be embarrassed by it. Speak of humanity as the crowning jewel of creation and you will very quickly be met with accusations of arrogance and hubris.

"How can you possibly think that we are the crowning jewel of creation when we are simply the next rung on the evolutionary ladder?"

"Given the odds there are certainly more advanced beings than us living on distant planets. How could we possibly think we are so special?"

How indeed?

The answer comes from God. When God decided to make the final piece of creation He made it clear that this would be the ultimate piece, the one that did something no other part of creation could do. Humanity would represent God in the world. It would be made in His very image.

Over the centuries there have been all sorts of ideas about what it means to be made in God's image. Some have focused on how God is a relational being and therefore so are we. Others have emphasized the moral nature or rational aspects of God and looked for those things in us. Then there is always the caveat that the fall and human sin have damaged that image. All of these things need to be part of the discussion. But they are hardly provocative. In order to really see how radical God was in the creation of human beings in His image we need to grasp the context of Genesis 1.

I regularly teach a class at Northland on Sunday mornings. You don't need to be a student there for very long before you will hear how important context is. Anytime you deal with a passage from the Bible you must never take it in isolation. It sits in the middle of other passages that have a huge impact on the meaning and application of the text. Those verses sit within a paragraph, within a chapter, a book, a testament, and the whole of the Bible. On top of all that is the historical context of the first author and readers. We need to understand what the author meant and what the first hearers/readers understood the passage to mean. The Bible was written for us, but it was written to them, the first audience.

When Genesis 1:26-27 says that we are made in the image and likeness of God, we need to ask, What did that mean to the people who first read those words? It helps to consider other places where they heard about images and likenesses. For that we need look no further than the Ten Commandments: *"You shall have no other gods before me. You shall not make for yourself a carved image or any likeness of anything that is in heaven above or the earth beneath"* (Exodus 20:3-4a).

The people who first heard about being made in God's image/likeness were also the people who first heard that they were never to make an image or likeness of anything that could take the place of God in their lives. They were to have no image/likeness that they would worship as a false god. Surely the similarity in the language of Genesis 1:16-27 and Exodus 20:3-4 would not have been lost on them. Something similar was being said about them being the image/likeness of God and the forbidden image/likeness of false gods.

In our supposed twenty-first-century sophistication we dismiss any notion of physical idols or images as having any real significance. We see them only as a tangible focal point of something purely spiritual. The Native American totem pole is just wood. The Greek statue of Aphrodite is just stone. In our minds there is no reality to what they represent. But to the people of the Bible and the cultures in biblical lands, the image, statue, or carving was far more than mere stone or wood. It was in some way, albeit a subsidiary way, the thing it represented. When people would bow down to an image of Baal, they were in fact bowing down to Baal who was by proxy present in the statue. The image in some way acted in the place of the original. To worship the image was to worship the original. To reject the image was to reject the original.

In 1 Samuel 5, the Philistines have captured the Ark of the Covenant. They haul it off to Ashdod and place it in the temple of their god, Dagon. In the morning they enter the temple and the statue of Dagon has fallen and is literally on its face before the Ark. When we read this chapter we need to take careful notice of the fact that it doesn't say "the statue of Dagon fell down before the Ark." It says, "Behold, Dagon had fallen face downward on the ground before the Ark of the Lord" (1 Samuel 5:4). This didn't happen just one morning but two mornings in a row. The second time, we are told, the head and hands of Dagon were cut off and tossed aside with only the torso of Dagon left where he had fallen. The image of Dagon in some way stood in proxy for Dagon himself. When the image fell down before the Ark, it meant Dagon had fallen in submission before the Ark of the Lord. When the hands and head of the statue were cut off and tossed aside it meant that in some way the hands and head of Dagon were cut off and tossed aside. As a result the Philistines acknowledged that the God of Israel was more powerful than Dagon and they quickly sent the Ark away.

When God said that He was going to make us in His image, it meant that we were created in order to stand in for God in some way. We were made to represent God in creation. Just as the Philistines saw the statue/image of Dagon as acting on behalf of, in proxy for, Dagon, so the Israelites would have understood that humanity as a whole was created in the image/likeness of God to act on behalf of, in proxy for, God in creation. When we look at one another we should be struck by the amazing realization that "we see God people." We see people who represent God to the world and act on His behalf. God doesn't need us to represent Him in the world, but by His grace He chose to give us the dignity of being His image-bearers and the crowning jewel of His creation.

So what is our role? In what way are we to stand in for God as His image-bearers? We get the first indication of an answer in the second half of verse 26: "... and let them rule over the fish of the sea and the birds of the sky and over the cattle and over all the earth." We were made in God's image in order to be God's representatives in ruling over and being stewards of creation. Contrary to popular opinion, the world's oldest profession is not prostitution. It is gardening. We were made by God to be His representatives, caring for the creation that He made.

So what are the implications of us bearing the image/likeness of God and being given the responsibility to rule over creation? Keeping in mind that the ultimate goal is to glorify God, there are at least three serious implications for how we live. The first has gained more notice in recent years after centuries of neglect. We must be careful stewards of creation and care for it in a way that honors God. It is puzzling to me that Christians have not led the way in the proper care and stewardship of Creation. After all, it is fundamental to the reason God has created us in His image. Granted, there are all sorts of creation worshipers who are part of the environmental movement. But the existence of misguided people caring for God's creation should not be a reason for Christians to avoid the earliest responsibility God gave us.

Second, how we live in relation to God as His image-bearers should be something that honors Him. When we fall into sin, we dishonor God. As His image-bearers, if our reputation is tarnished then by association so is God's. Our lives should be lived in such a way as to worship God in all we do. We are made for His glory and so we should live like it.

Thirdly, and the implication I wish to expand upon, is that as image/likeness-bearers we are the most tangible expression of God that most people will ever see. Like it or not, many if not most people will make a decision about the validity of our faith and of following Christ not on the basis of our doctrinal purity, but on the basis of the holiness of our lives. What they see in us as His image-bearers is what they will think of God.

In the 1970s there was a television commercial in America that showed a boy of about five in a crowded airport. He was carrying a box full of puzzle pieces. In all the hustle and bustle someone knocked into the little boy and he dropped the box, spilling puzzle pieces all over the floor. Busy travelers didn't even notice as the child was on the floor, desperately trying to gather all the pieces into the box. Suddenly a shadow loomed over him as a middle-aged businessman stooped down and helped the boy gather all the pieces into the box. At the end the boy looked up at the man and asked, "Are you God?" That is what it means to be an image/likeness-bearer.

People should be able to look at Christians and see God. If that makes you a bit uncomfortable, wondering if I am not going off some New Age deep end where we all become one with God and become God, I understand your concern. But let's consider this from a strictly New Testament perspective. In 1 Corinthians 12 we find the image of us as the body and Christ as the head of the church. Paul also tells us in 1 Corinthians 9 that we are ambassadors of Christ, representing Him to the world. We are told that we are to grow into maturity in all things becoming like Christ (Ephesians 4:15). In John 17:18-21, Jesus prays that we would be one as He and the Father are one, and as He prays to the Father he makes this startling statement:

"As you sent me into the world, so I have sent them into the world. And for their sake I consecrate myself, that they also may be sanctified in truth. I do not ask for these only, but also for those who will believe in me through their word, that they may all be one, just as you, Father, are in me, and I in you, that they also may be in us, so that the world may believe that you have sent me."

Jesus prays that His followers, even those who were not yet born, would be one just as He and the Father are one. He also prays that we would be "in" them—that is, so united to the Father and the Son that when people see us, they would see them. Just as the Father sent Jesus into the world so people would see the Father, Jesus sends us into the world so people would see them both. That is redemption at its finest. It is redeeming the original mission God gave us when He created us in His image.

All of this points to the fact that when God declared that humanity would be made in His image, that we in some way became God's representatives in the world. More than that, we became God's agents in the world to act on His behalf. When God said that those who were made in His image would also have dominion over the earth, He was giving us a charge to rule in His name. We are stewards of God. We function in His name, on His behalf, for His glory. What we say and do as image-bearers, we do with the authority of God and for His glory. We represent Him.

It is what Paul speaks about in 1 Corinthians 5 when he says that we are ambassadors for Christ. As ambassadors, we stand in place of and speak on behalf of our sovereign Lord. When people see us act and hear us speak, they should be confident that this is how the sovereign Lord would speak and act if he was present. In Colossians 3:17 Paul says, *"And whatever you do, in word or deed, do everything in the name of the Lord Jesus, giving thanks to God the Father through him."*

There are at least two important points Paul is making here. One is that as image-bearers of Jesus, everything we do reflects back on Him. When people see us they should in some way expect to see Jesus. Second, our acting and our speaking should be done in such a way as to bring glory to Jesus.

Being an image/likeness-bearer of God is a heavy responsibility. It seems crazy on God's part to entrust to us the representation of Him to the world. It seems ridiculous for Him to entrust to us the power and authority to be His stewards over all creation, acting in His name and on His behalf. It seems comical that God would entrust to us the responsibility of building a society and culture that glorifies Him above all else. But that is exactly what He has done. He has created us in His image. We are his representatives, stewards, vice-regents if you will. When people see us, they should see something of the glory of God.

One of the most powerful books you can read, outside the Bible, is Dietrich Bonhoeffer's *The Cost of Discipleship*. Bonhoeffer was a dedicated follower of Jesus who paid the price of his life for His love of Jesus. He was executed by the Nazis in the closing days of World War II. Clearly, he understood and paid the cost of discipleship. In that book he makes this incredible observation of how followers of Jesus are His image-bearers to the world. Speaking of Jesus sending His followers out in His name, Bonhoeffer writes:

> *"They are now Christ's fellow-workers, and will be like Him in all things. Thus they are to meet those to whom they are sent as if they were Christ Himself. When they are welcomed into a house, Christ enters with them. They are bearers of His presence. They bring with them the most precious gift in the world, the gift of Jesus Christ. And with Him they bring the Father."*

Bonhoeffer is spot on. When Christ-followers go into the world they do so bearing His image and bringing Him wherever they go. When people receive them into their world and space, they receive Jesus.

We don't need to be embarrassed by that, or apologize for what God has determined to do. But we do need to get on with the mission of representing Him differently. We need to represent Him so that He is indeed glorified in us and we are enjoying Him forever. For that we will need to become far more provocative, in a biblical sense, than we currently are. In fact we will need to become provocative like the first several generations of Christ-followers.

CHAPTER 2

YOU'RE NOT OK, AND NEITHER AM I!

*"We have all become like one who is unclean,
and all our righteous deeds are like a polluted garment.
We all fade like a leaf,
and our iniquities, like the wind, take us away."* — Isaiah 64:6

*"Therefore, just as sin came into the world through one man, and death
through sin, and so death spread to all men because all sinned."*
— Romans 5:12

"Everything that used to be a sin is now a disease." — Bill Maher

"I'm OK, it's the rest of the world that's all horsed up." — Chuck Stauffer

IN A WONDERFUL SCENE in the movie, *Toy Story,* a group of toys accuse Woody, the cowboy action figure, of something that he didn't do. Convinced of his wrongdoing and betrayal of the group they toss him off the back of a moving van as it speeds down the road. Upon realization of their error, the somewhat neurotic plastic T-Rex whines, "Great. Now I have guilt." He is not alone. Ever since Adam and Eve sinned against God, human beings have been wrestling with the realization that we have guilt.

Through the millennia we have tried all sorts of methods to alleviate our feelings of guilt. It started with Adam and Eve. Even though they had been made in the image of God, serving as His representatives to the world, that was not enough. Instead they decided they didn't want to be in the image of God, they wanted to be equal to God. So they reached for that which had been forbidden them. No, it wasn't an apple as popular notions would have it. What was forbidden them was the knowledge of good and evil and the fruit of that tree. The serpent told them that it would make them "like God." The temptation was too great. The desire to be something they were not created to be drove them. They were not satisfied or content to be the crowning jewel of creation, image-bearers of God. They wanted to supplant God and be His equal.

Immediately upon reaching for what they never could have, they experienced guilt and shame. Their efforts to deal with that guilt are found in their first, comical attempts to hide from an omniscient, omnipresent God. They hid behind the bushes hoping against hope that God would not see their nakedness. They suddenly felt very exposed because of their guilt and shame. Our attempts to overcome our feelings of guilt and shame have progressed, or maybe regressed, over the centuries. Our most recent effort is to deny that we have anything to feel guilty about. As comedian and talk show host Bill Maher points out, we have turned everything that used to be sin into a disease. If you have a disease, then it's not your fault and you have nothing to feel guilty about. If that doesn't work for us, then we do our best to believe what my friend Chuck Stauffer used to say, *"I'm OK, it's the rest of the world that's all horsed up."* You have to have known Chuck to know that he was being sarcastic more than anything. Chuck was one of the most godly men I ever knew, yet he was also brutally aware of his own sin and shortcomings, while at the same time being gracious and forgiving towards everyone else.

I include Chuck's bit of sarcasm because I know that for most people, myself included, we try to deny our own guilt, oftentimes by pointing out how bad other people are. Typically we find someone, or a group of someones, we determine to be worse than we are. We know we are not as good as Billy Graham or Francis of Assisi, but we take comfort in not being as bad as the Nazis or KKK members or Al Qaeda suicide bombers. So we see ourselves as being about average and hope God grades on a curve and that we are good enough to get into heaven.

Yet in spite of all our efforts to justify ourselves and convince ourselves that we really are OK—even if the rest of the world, or at least half of it, is more horsed up than we are—people still live with the incredible weight of guilt and shame. In fact, you can make the case that our growing fascination with self-help books, the increasing numbers of people in counseling, and the angst that people feel are all indicators of our inability to deal with real guilt. Something inside us will not let us accept the psychological mind games that we play to deny that we are flawed. For all the positive-thinking books we read, and all the "you are wonderful" pep talks we hear, people still wrestle with the awareness that they are not what they ought to be or want to be. When push comes to shove people are forced to admit that we human beings are truly broken inside and we are not as good as we think we are.

I came to Christ at the very end of my junior year in high school. Fortunately during my senior year I was discipled by a great guy named Scott Jones. Scott was the leader of the local Young Life club. At the beginning of my senior year we began meeting each Wednesday morning, along with a half-dozen other guys, to study Paul's letter to the Romans. During that time I was in an English class, really more of a literature class that was an excuse to talk about all sorts of interesting topics. The teacher presented a question to the class one day, as we were seated at our desks in a large circle: "Is there anything that is true all the time?" My mind immediately went to the passage from Romans that we had studied just recently, *"All have sinned and fallen short of the glory of God."* And yes, I spoke up and quoted Romans 3:23 in my high school English class. Seated across the circle from me was a girl who was the shot-putter on the girl's track team. She leaned forward in her desk, bore a hole through me with her stare and said, "What do you mean by sin?" It was game on, and again I was thankful for that discipleship group. My response was that sin could be defined, as "believing that something is wrong and doing it anyway." I will never forget how her head did this little tilt to one side, her face suddenly relaxed, and she said, "Oh, OK. That makes sense."

What I got from that exchange is we humans have this revulsion to the idea that we are sinners. We don't want to admit it. We are ready to come up out of our chair and argue for our innate purity and goodness. We want to believe the title of the best-selling book, *I'm OK, You're OK.* But we are not "OK" and we know it. When someone makes a simple statement like, "We all do things that we know are wrong," we are forced to agree, "That makes sense." Why? Because it takes but a nanosecond to be confronted with our own peccadilloes and faults. They are lying just below the surface of our carefully constructed web of denial. And all it takes is someone pointing out that we all do stuff we know is wrong and we are forced to admit our brokenness and need. C. S. Lewis put it this way: *"All men alike stand condemned, not by alien codes of ethics, but by their own, and all men therefore are conscious of guilt."*

You would think once we are willing to admit we all sin that then we would finally be ready to deal with this most serious of human conditions. But our cleverness in avoiding the ramifications of our actions is strong. As soon as people become convinced that they in fact do sin and that we all sin, we decide that sin is not that serious. After all, the thinking goes, since everyone sins how bad can it be? If we are all sinners, doesn't that somehow mean that on average we are all the same? So we end up assuaging our guilt by deciding that we are just like everyone else and so it's not that bad. As the saying goes, "To err is human." So sin now becomes "normal," and if it is normal, then don't sweat it.

We effectively lower the bar by saying since we all sin; God must at least wink at us average sinners and give us a free pass. God can't possibly be angry with people who are just being average sinners. If He must do something about sin, punish it in some way, then it should be reserved for the really bad sinners: Hitler, Stalin, Jack the Ripper, those kinds of people.

The point of Romans 3:23 is not to make us feel secure in the company of eight billion other sinners. It is not so we decide that since we all sin, then it's normal, therefore acceptable. The point is to let us know that nobody is free from the guilt and implications of sin and that our situation is deadly serious.

A little later in his letter to the Romans, Paul puts forth the deadly consequences of our sin:

"Therefore, just as sin came into the world through one man, and death through sin, and so death spread to all men because all sinned" (Romans 5:12).

It should come as no surprise that death is the outcome of our sin. God said it would be so. He told Adam and Eve not to eat of the tree of the knowledge of good and evil: If they did, they would surely die. Some have looked at Genesis 2:17 and decided that it is not true, that something is amiss because Adam and Eve did not die immediately. But God wasn't saying that they would drop dead on the spot, struck down by swift and deadly divine retribution. What He said was that they would die as a result of tasting from that tree. If they had never eaten from that tree, they would have never died! Human death did not exist prior to them violating God's command. They would have continued to live in the garden with God, in perfect peace for all eternity. Because Adam and Eve did violate God's command, they forced a fundamental shift in the human experience.

Wrapped up in this discussion of sin are two extremely provocative things God has said. The first is that all of us are by our very nature sinners in rebellion against God. We are at war with God. The second is we don't just have an illness or a disease that makes us sick, something that we can psychologize away or from which we can therapeutically fix ourselves. We have a nature that makes us spiritually dead and puts us on an unswerving path to a date with the Grim Reaper, where we will face physical death and whatever eternal fate awaits us.

It is that sinful nature which is at the root of our spiritual dysfunction. During the Enlightenment, philosopher John Locke proposed the idea that human beings are born with a blank slate. According to Locke, our problem is a lack of education. We are born ignorant of the information we need. That blank slate is not just an intellectual one but also a moral/spiritual one. Contrary to what the Bible teaches, Locke's philosophy and its subsequent adherents would say that we are born innocent, guiltless, without sin, and all we need to live a good life is the right kind of training and moral upbringing that will put the proper ideas and subsequent behaviors on our blank slate. Locke would argue that we do not have a predisposition to sin. Instead we sin, do wrong things, because we have not been educated effectively.

In the latter part of the nineteenth and early part of the twentieth centuries there was a pervasive positive attitude in the Western world. Humanity was becoming more educated and sophisticated. Science was leading the way in solving a myriad of man's problems. Locke's philosophy was playing out as true. As long as we educated people correctly and put the right thinking on the blank slate, then we could create a utopian world. All of that came crashing down on the fields of Flanders and other parts of Europe in WWI. In little over four years, from July 28, 1914 to November 11, 1918, more than fifteen million people were killed and another twenty million wounded. That "war to end all wars" turned out to simply be the prelude to even more unimaginable global butchery. Twenty years later humanity once again tried to tear itself to shreds, and nearly succeeded. In all, sixty million people were killed in World War II. Sixty million! That would be one out of every five Americans alive today. In World War II the Nazi concentration camps alone accounted for nearly as many deaths as in all of World War I.

The thing that made the atrocities of World War II so disturbing was that so many "normal" people engaged in such despicable acts. It wasn't possible for a handful of psychotic sociopaths to kill fourteen million people in concentration camps without help. Thousands of average, everyday, normal, hard-working, seemingly moral people also had a hand in making that happen. The Rape of Nanking, China, occurred when Imperial Japanese soldiers occupied the city in 1938. Estimates vary but go as high as eighty thousand women being raped and three hundred thousand people executed. Even if the numbers are half those estimates, it was a brutal atrocity. Shockingly it was the work of thousands of soldiers who prior to the war lived peaceful lives, caring for their families, bouncing their children on their knees, and trimming their bonsai trees in peaceful zen gardens. The list of brutality goes on ad infinitum up to the present day: something in us is easily twisted to evil.

Locke's idea that we are born with a blank slate has proved foolish at best and dangerous at worst. The more educated we get, the more creative we get in our ability to damage one another. Something inside us is broken. When we look at ourselves in the mirror of inner reflection we often find things we don't like, demons we want to keep hidden. It is rather like the quote from C. S. Lewis: *"Education without morals, as useful as it is, rather seems to make man a more clever devil."* The more educated we get, without having God at the core, means that we just get more efficient at destroying one another. We do so because our nature as people is in rebellion against God, in other words our default mode is to sin and sin wildly, horrifically, tragically. We do so even when a part of us doesn't want to.

The Apostle Paul, one of the most disciplined men to ever take a breath, put it this way:

"For I do not understand my own actions. For I do not do what I want, but I do the very thing I hate. Now if I do what I do not want, I agree with the law, that it is good. ... For I know that nothing good dwells in me, that is, in my flesh. For I have the desire to do what is right, but not the ability to carry it out. For I do not do the good I want, but the evil I do not want is what I keep on doing" (Romans 7:15-16, 18-19).

One final point needs to be made concerning our predilection to sin. We have the notion that we are sinners because we sin. In other words, you are not a sinner until you commit some overt act of sinning. But that fails to explain why we sin. It offers no explanation for where the motivation for such an act came from. Instead of thinking that we are sinners because we sin, we need to come to grips with the idea that we sin because we are sinners. We do that which comes from within our nature. We are people who have rebelled against God and by nature are prone to sinful things. We are born this way. It is indigenous to who we are. The amazing thing should not be that we sin, but rather that with such a rebellious nature we do anything good at all.

You were not born as Locke's clean slate. You were born as one who was self-centered, rebellious, and an enemy of God. That predisposition eventually showed itself in your behavior. As an "innocent" two-year-old you reared back and hammered your playmate who happened to pick up the toy you wanted to play with, in spite of the fact that your mother regularly tried to fill your "clean slate" with ideas of cooperation and sharing.

You sinned against your playmate because at the core you are a sinner. It's who we are and what we do best. We are proficient in sin because it is our nature. It was evident at two years of age and is still evident no matter the number of years you have trod this earthen ball, and no matter how educated and sophisticated you have become.

CHAPTER 3

HELPLESS BUT NOT HOPELESS

"God helps those who help themselves." — Poor Richard's Almanack

"For by grace you have been saved through faith. And this is not your own doing; it is the gift of God, not a result of works, so that no one may boast."
— Ephesians 2:8-9

"Since then we have a great high priest who has passed through the heavens, Jesus, the Son of God, let us hold fast our confession. ... Let us then with confidence draw near to the throne of grace, that we may receive mercy and find grace to help in time of need." — Hebrews 4:14,16

T WAS AT THE first Bible study I can ever recall. I was there because of Holly Travis. She was a girl I had asked out on a date for the coming Friday and her response was, "That would be great. There is a Bible study at my friend Amy's house on Wednesday, would you like to come to that?" I didn't see that coming, not by a long shot. But if I wanted the Friday date, I figured that I had to go to the Wednesday Bible study. It was a Bible study called Campaigners, part of the Young Life ministry to high school students. That was were I met Scott Jones, my first mentor in my relationship with Christ. Scott said something that caught my attention. In essence it was that the only way that we can have eternal life is because God gives it as a gift that we accept by faith, and that we can't do anything to earn a place in heaven. To my admittedly limited religious understanding that just seemed wrong. Everything I ever understood was that

43

you had to do enough good stuff to make sure you got to heaven. Somehow forgiveness was involved for the really huge stuff that we did and felt sorry for, but ultimately you had to have more good-deed chips in your stack than bad-deed chips. Of course you could never really know how many of either kind of chip you had in either pile. So, to mix a few metaphors, you hoped that God graded on a curve and that you were a better person than the average sinner. At the very least you took comfort in the fact that you were not as bad as Hitler, who certainly must be in hell. All of that made getting into heaven something of a gamble that you could never really be sure about.

What was certain was that you got into heaven by being good enough to get let in; it was really all up to you. But here was Scott Jones saying that heaven was a free gift given to us simply if we trusted in Jesus. Not being one who has ever been shy about speaking up, even when I am not really sure what I am talking about, I graciously objected. "Wait a minute," I said with something of a question in my voice. "Doesn't the Bible say, 'God helps those who help themselves'?" Yep, I really did quote that as coming from the Bible. What did I know? It was my first Bible study. Well, after the more experienced church-going types had a laugh, Holly kindly leaned over and said, "That's from *Poor Richard's Almanack*. Benjamin Franklin said that." My reply was something lame like, "Well, it sounds like it should be in the Bible."

I learned two things from that encounter. One was that salvation is all about grace and nothing about me being good enough to earn heaven. The second was something that has also stuck with me ever since. Christians are terrible at making people who do not understand the Bible or Christianity feel at ease. Everyone but Holly and Scott got a laugh out of my ignorance, or at least it felt that way. I eventually came to faith in Christ in large part due to Holly's graciousness, and vowed that I would always seek to treat non-believers with dignity and respect in order to win them to the King.

As to the idea that salvation is totally by grace, I have since found that it is something that most Christians believe intellectually and state as a central doctrine, but they don't really live as if it is true. If you observed and listened to what many Christians say and do, when not asked for a Sunday School answer about salvation, you would quickly determine that, functionally, when it comes to salvation most people are closer to *Poor Richard's Almanack* than they are to Ephesians 2:8-9. Several surveys I have seen over the years have consistently shown that a majority of people who claim a relationship of faith with Jesus still think that their works have something to do with getting them into heaven.

On the one hand that should be shocking, since the Bible is so bold and clear about salvation by grace. On the other hand it is not at all a surprise when we consider the bigger picture of the human condition. There is something in us that universally wants to place our eternal destiny in our own hands and ability to achieve an eternal reward. It is so ingrained in us that even when we are told in a straightforward way that salvation is not of works, so that no one can boast, we still revert to the default mode of trying to be good enough to earn it.

I once taught a semester class on world religions for a local high school. We studied the basic history, customs, and doctrines of Hinduism, Buddhism, Judaism, Christianity, and Islam. One of the things common to all those religions, and religions in general, is that they ask the question, What happens when you die? The answer in each case eventually involves some notion of a paradise or state of eternal bliss or oneness with the universe. The details are radically different from religion to religion, but in principle they all have us looking to some future that is to be more desired than what we have now. In some cases there is also a future of eternal punishment that is not to be desired—Christianity, Judaism, Islam—or there is a cycle of rebirth into this world that is also not desirable since the goal is to escape this world—Hinduism, Buddhism. Ideally, though, you are wanting to have an eternal destiny that is positive and blessed according to that religion's standards.

One day we did a comparison chart of the basic beliefs of each religion. One of the comparisons was how each thought you reached the eternal goal. What was stunning for students to see on the whiteboard was that four of the five—Hinduism, Buddhism, Judaism, and Islam—all had personal effort and work as the basic way to reach the goal. In each case you achieved what was necessary to spend eternity in whatever the blissful state was. It didn't matter whether it was Nirvana for the Buddhist, or Paradise for the Muslim; it was up to you to make it happen. The difference was Christianity. In that case, eternal blessing was achieved not by fulfilling a list of laws or regulations, nor by being overly devoted to meditation and fasting. Instead it was a gift. It was something given by God as a result of faith in Jesus Christ. But even that faith was a gift, not something we figured out and came up with all by ourselves.

The truth is, you could do that same comparison chart for religion after religion after religion. I have yet to come up with one that has salvation based in anything other than our human effort, except Christianity. It seems that deep within us, including me at that first Bible study, is this desire to in some way lay claim to being able to achieve the unachievable. There is a pride, a human hubris, that wants to leave God out of the equation. Religion after religion says you must do something and you can do something to achieve the eternal goal. Only Christianity says that whatever you try to do will always fall short. Only Christianity says that God has provided a way forward, a way marked by grace and grace alone.

Salvation by grace is certainly something provocative, if the definition of provocative is something that provokes or compels a response. Whenever I talk about salvation by grace alone there are two universal responses that the discussion provokes. The first is that it can't be that easy. Grace just seems too good to be true. People are so convinced that they must be good enough to get into heaven that the message of God's grace is hard to accept. That response is the previously mentioned hubris raising its ugly head in one last desperate gasp, trying with all its power to convince us that we are in control and we are going to rise up to the level of God.

I understand that response. The religious world around us is constantly promoting the idea that you have to be a good person for God to accept you. Even within Christianity there is a sizable contingent that speaks of salvation by grace but then acts as if it is all about being good enough. Countless preachers give sermon after sermon that is a version of biblical moralism. They find things the Bible says to do or not do and those become the focus of the sermon. If you are a good Christian you will do these things—pray, read your Bible, tithe, go on a mission trip—and not do these things—watch R-rated movies, drink, smoke, dance, or chew, or go out with girls who do. Pretty soon people get the idea that to be a Christian and acceptable to God is all about doing good stuff and not doing bad stuff. So when someone comes along and says, "No! Salvation is a gracious gift from God and you cannot earn it," it just seems too incredible. Salvation as a free gift from God is intended to be provocative. God wants us to react, to be stunned, to be overwhelmed, and even a bit incredulous. He wants to get our attention and force us to react, one way or another.

The second response I often see is normally in the form of a question: "So if you are right in saying that it doesn't matter what you do, that being good enough doesn't get us into heaven, that it is only by grace, then why can't I just believe in Jesus and then go off and do whatever in the world I want because God will just forgive me?" What I like about that question is that at least the message of salvation as a free gift has come across as provocative. It has led to an honest question that leads to a dialogue on a real issue. If God forgives us freely, then why wouldn't I just keep asking forgiveness and do whatever I want? After all, wouldn't God be required to let me into heaven and forgive me?

This is where the oft-ignored and sometimes belittled letter of James comes in. Martin Luther was not a fan: he infamously called it "the epistle of straw." Luther's problem with James was that he thought it smacked of salvation by works. Given Luther's aversion to anything that seemed like works righteousness, I suppose we can understand and forgive his over-reaction to James. What James was actually addressing was the very notion stated in the previous question: "Since I am saved by grace, why can't I just sin in anyway I wish and then be forgiven?" James helps us to understand that although salvation is by grace alone through faith, it is not by grace or faith that is alone.

James deals with the issue this way. People had been boasting about their faith. The problem was, their faith was not evident in anything other than their boasting. Their lives simply did not show that they really believed in and loved Jesus. James was concerned that their faith was not of the saving sort, but was rather nothing more than an intellectual understanding of Jesus, who He was and what He did. That, according to James, was a recipe for disaster. To believe only intellectually that Jesus is the Lord God come in the flesh, and not to love Him and trust Him with your salvation, only qualifies you to be a demon. You have no more understanding of and relationship with Jesus than the average demon. Demons know who Jesus is and they know what He is all about. They demonstrated that when Jesus began to cast them out of a man. They cried out, "We know who you are, Son of the Most High, and we know why you are here." According to James, people who know who Jesus is and why He came, and believe it to be true, have met all the faith qualifications to be a demon.

Rather than giving evidence of one's faith by simply spouting off about it, James said that he would give evidence of his faith by what he did, by the changed life that was a result of his faith. Demons might have intellectual belief in who Jesus is, but they did not have saving faith that was combined with repentance and a changed life. It was here that he made the famous statement, "Faith without works is dead" (James 2:26).

Saving faith that has its source in God's grace will result in a love for Jesus that will motivate you to live differently. I will desire to live in obedience to all that Jesus has commanded. In some ways that life may even look exactly like the person who is striving under their own power to be good. The difference is in the motivation, the relationship of love you have for Jesus. The person who has been saved by grace, having his or her sins freely forgiven, will be a person who has a love for Christ that grows more and more. That love for Christ is what motivates living differently.

It is common for people today to go forward at a church service and pray a prayer to "accept" Jesus into their hearts. We need to be extremely careful that we don't give people the idea that they have now punched their ticket to heaven as a result. Such a step should be seen as the first in a lifelong relationship with Christ. It is the beginning, not the end. Yes, your salvation is a free gift from Jesus. But if you truly have faith, then you will live in an ongoing relationship with Him, following Him, loving Him, serving Him. The salvation is free. But the life you live as a result of that free gift should bind you to Jesus and cause you to live as if your entire salvation depended on living in obedience to Him.

As I was nearing the final few chapters of this book I had a very long conversation with a woman who had been attending Northland Church for only a few weeks. Nine months prior she had stopped attending a local Mormon congregation, after eight years of extreme devotion and adherence to the teachings and practices of Mormonism. She was wrestling with the tension she felt between a Christianity that was about a relationship with Jesus who loved her, and Mormonism, which played on her deeply ingrained idea that she had to be good enough for God to accept her.

On the one hand she had a very real sense that she was a sinner and not perfect. Something needed to be done about that so she could get closer to God. Mormonism told her that if she did a whole host of endless religious activities and was obedient in the extreme, becoming perfect, then maybe, just maybe she would achieve an incredible eternal existence as a cosmic princess. The problem was, she could never know for sure if she had arrived, had done all that was required. There always seemed to be more to do, and her sense of feeling unworthy never went away. If anything it increased. In spite of all her striving, she never knew if she did enough for God to love her.

On the other hand she was beginning to understand that she could not do all that was needed to become perfectly acceptable to God, and in fact didn't have to. Jesus had done for her what she could not. Why? Because He already loved her. Jesus died for her because He loved her, not so she would be forced into a works-righteousness bondage in which she tried to convince God to love her. Her striving to gain God's love was so totally unnecessary and in fact served to keep her isolated from God's love. The harder she worked to earn God's love the less she actually experienced it and the further she wandered from it.

This realization that God loved her, in spite of her sin and not because of her efforts at being righteous, put her in the early stages of a spiritual tug of war. Pulling on one end of the rope was the guilt-driven idea that you need to work harder and harder to be acceptable to God. Pulling on the other end was the biblical truth that God loves you and Christ died for you because of that love, and all your striving for personal perfection is counter-productive.

As she continues to get closer to God through a relationship of grace, she is learning that the motivation for righteous living is not to earn God's love, but rather because she has already been a recipient of the incredible, immeasurable love of God that demonstrated itself when Jesus went to the cross for her.

CHAPTER 4

JESUS: GOOD MAN OR GOD-MAN?

"'Your father Abraham rejoiced that he would see my day. He saw it and was glad.' So the Jews said to him, 'You are not yet fifty years old, and have you seen Abraham?' Jesus said to them, 'Truly, truly, I say to you, before Abraham was, I am.' So they picked up stones to throw at him, but Jesus hid himself and went out of the temple."
— John 8:56-59

" 'If you had known me, you would have known my Father also. From now on you do know him and have seen him.' " — John 14:7

"A man who was merely a man and said the sort of things Jesus said would not be a great moral teacher. He would either be a lunatic—on a level with the man who says he is a poached egg—or else he would be the Devil of Hell. You must make your choice. Either this man was, and is, the Son of God; or else a madman or something worse." — C.S. Lewis

S O YOU KNOW YOU are made in God's image. You know that as a result of sin that image is tainted, your relationship broken, and you are destined to eternal punishment. That is about as bad as news can get. But you also know the Good News that, because of God's love and mercy, He has made available to you the free gift of salvation and eternal life. He grants it as a gift to all who believe and trust in Jesus as their Lord and Savior, following Him. When you think on those two things—your utter sinfulness and God's act of redeeming love through the sacrificial death of His son—you begin to experience how provocative our God is. You also begin to see that Jesus is at the center of this provocativeness.

But just who or what is Jesus? What makes Jesus so special? Shockingly, the answer is that Jesus is God Himself. He came into the world and took on humanity. He left the glorious joy and ecstasy of heaven and He became one of us. He is the God-man. He is God incarnate. The word "incarnate" is related to one we are all familiar with, "carne." Chili con carne is, in my opinion, the only real way to make chili. It means chili with meat. Forget that vegetarian chili, give me some meat! The same is true when it comes to Jesus. The doctrine of the incarnation means that God took on flesh, meat, skin and bone, muscle and sinew. I don't want some ephemeral Jesus who floats two inches above the ground, moving as some untouchable spirit who will not soil His feet by touching a fallen world. Give me God in the flesh. Give me Jesus the God-man.

It has become fashionable of late to argue that the Bible never claims that Jesus is God. People state that Jesus never makes any claim to be God. They say He never claims to be divine. Of course that begs the question, "If that is true, then how in the world did the divinity of Jesus become a foundational doctrine of Christianity?" The common assertion that Jesus never claimed divinity is something that fits nicely in our age of conspiracy theories and rewriting history to suit our preconceived notions. As the conspiracy theory goes, Jesus never claimed to be anything more than a spiritually enlightened moral teacher who was demonstrating the way of love. He got caught up in the machinery of the power brokers of His day and was executed for being a social, political, religious revolutionary. More than three hundred years later, the new power broker, the Emperor Constantine, needed to unite the empire and made use of the church to do so. He forced a council of bishops at Nicaea to come up with some unifying doctrine for all the empire—not unlike the modern physicists' quest for a Grand Unifying Theory that will unite all scientific understanding and explain everything. The conspiracy surrounding Nicaea and Constantine claims that this council decided that Jesus was divine not based on Scripture, but created the belief on the spot. As the conspiracy theory goes, the church then went on to suppress and persecute anyone and anything that taught a doctrine of Jesus other than this newly-constructed Constantinian one.

People with a personal need for Jesus to not be divine quickly grab at this idea. The result has been a whole cottage industry purporting to have evidence of this conspiracy to make Jesus divine when He was not. People who should know better ignore the facts of history and take it all in as truth, just like the latest Oliver Stone movie reconstruction of history. I was especially struck by how far this idea has spread when I saw a recent retelling of the story of King Arthur in a Hollywood movie. Clive Owen plays Arthur, who is a Christian fighting for Rome in England. He is a follower of a branch of Christianity that loves Jesus but does not hold to His divinity. Those who are connected to the established church in Rome and hold to the divinity of Christ are depicted as corrupt and evil men who use their doctrines to keep people in bondage. Arthur, on the other hand, is the very model of the person of integrity, love, sacrifice, and grace, following in the footsteps of Jesus the great teacher. I know there are lots of variations of the Arthur myth, but this was the first time that I saw Arthur being used as a not-so-subtle statement supporting the conspiracy theory of a corrupt church using the doctrines of the person of Christ to keep people in bondage.

The reality is that Constantine was not nearly the bogeyman that so many have made him out to be. He certainly did give Christianity a standing and legitimacy that it never had before in the Roman Empire. But he was far from the guy who created or forced the creation of a doctrine of Christ that made Jesus divine. That was not a notion that sprang to life at the Council of Nicaea in AD 324. There is plenty of evidence from the first to the third centuries that shows us how pre-Council of Nicaea Christians thought about and acted towards Jesus. Some crucial pieces of that evidence come from sources other than the Bible. Perhaps the most obvious is the statement of Pliny the Younger, the Roman governor of Bithynia in Asia Minor around AD 112. He wrote the following about Christians to Emperor Trajan:

"[The Christians] were in the habit of meeting on a certain fixed day before it was light, when they sang in alternate verses a hymn to Christ, as to a god..."

Pliny reported that the Christians at the turn of the first century were already worshiping Jesus as if He was "a god." That's more than two hundred years before Nicaea, and only a few years after the death of John, the last of the original apostles. Roman graffiti from this era has been found that mocks Christians for worshiping their God who is hanging on a cross. The Greek satirist Lucian also wrote in the second century, giving a rather detailed description of how Christians worshiped Jesus as their God. He did this in the style of the satirist ridiculing the "misguided creatures" who follow and worship a "crucified sage." Each of these examples points out that the earliest generation of Christians worshiped Jesus as one would worship God. Yet in spite of such well-known historical evidence—at least, it is well known among scholars of history and Christianity—supposedly intelligent, objective people swallow whole the myth that the fourth-century church made up the doctrine of Jesus' divinity.

Part of what I find fascinating and befuddling about this trend is that, in addition to rewriting history contrary to the evidence, it also completely ignores some of the most obvious and blatant claims to divinity by Jesus Himself. C.S. Lewis got it right with his quote at the opening of this chapter. Jesus is either a great liar, a lunatic on the same level of a man who claims to be a poached egg (only Lewis could come up with such a unique way to express something so important), or Jesus is something far more. When you look at what Jesus said and did you cannot possibly hold to the idea that He was simply some great moral teacher. You just don't have the option to believe that and still claim to be intellectually objective and fair.

I suppose that given the psychological state that goes along with unbelief it is to be expected that people will ignore evidence that is contrary to what they want to believe. It happens all the time. When it comes to Jesus and His divinity, there is a great deal on the line. If He is divine, then we must respond to Him with the devotion of our entire lives. Nothing short of complete and total dedication of our lives and love will do if Jesus is, in fact divine. That is a scary thought for most people. To be faced with giving yourself totally to the lordship and obedience of another, even Jesus, is not to be taken lightly. So I can cut some slack to the non-Christian who does not think Jesus is divine. I get that. If Jesus is acknowledged as divine, then it will toss their whole world into disarray. However, recently I have come across a growing number of people who claim to be Christians but do not think Jesus was God. I find that to be decidedly contradictory, sad, and a not a little bit frightening. They say they are Christians and really are trying to live for Jesus. Yet in no way do they think He was God.

On a certain level it really doesn't matter what they or even I think about Jesus being God. The real question is, "Did Jesus think that He was God?" The short answer to that question is clearly yes. In fact, that is precisely the reason why the religious leaders wanted to have Him crucified, and the real reason why the earliest Christians worship Him as such and called Him Lord.

As to Jesus being crucified because He claimed to be God, consider His encounter with the religious leaders in John 8:54-58:

> *"Jesus answered, 'If I glorify myself, my glory is nothing. It is my Father who glorifies me, of whom you say, "He is our God." But you have not known him. I know him. If I were to say that I do not know him, I would be a liar like you, but I do know him and I keep his word. Your father Abraham rejoiced that he would see my day. He saw it and was glad.' So the Jews said to him, 'You are not yet fifty years old, and have you seen Abraham?' Jesus said to them, 'Truly, truly, I say to you, before Abraham was, I am.' "*

Jesus claims that Abraham, who died nearly twenty centuries earlier, has actually seen and been seen by Jesus. The religious leaders mock Jesus by pointing out that he is not even fifty years old so there is no way He and Abraham can have seen one another. They are convinced that Jesus is a demon-possessed nutjob. Jesus responds by saying, "Before Abraham was born, I AM." Now that is certainly an odd way to respond. If Jesus is really God, why doesn't He understand basic grammar and the difference between past and present tense? What makes sense from a word-tense standpoint is for Jesus to say, "Before Abraham was born, I WAS." But He says, "I AM." At this point they pick up rocks in order to pummel and stone Him to death. Why?

The reason they want to kill Him right then and there is because they completely and clearly understand what Jesus has just said. By saying, "I AM," Jesus has just made the most provocative statement any of those learned religious leaders could ever imagine making. He has just committed blasphemy by claiming equality with God. In the eyes of those deeply religious men that is as sinful a thing as there could possibly be.

By using the term "I AM," instead of the grammatically correct "I WAS," Jesus is identifying Himself with God and the holiest of names used for God. He is reminding them of the name God used for Himself when He spoke to Moses on Mount Sinai, in Exodus 3. In that encounter Moses sees a bush that is burning but not consumed by the fire. A voice from the bush tells Moses that the cry of the people of Israel has been heard, and Moses is to go and free the people, as the representative of the God who is speaking from the bush. When Moses asks whom shall he say is the one who has sent him, he hears the name that God chooses to be identified with:

"God said to Moses, 'I am who I am.' And he said, 'Say this to the people of Israel, "I am has sent me to you."'" (Exodus 3:14).

That story and the name I AM was ingrained in the mind of every first-century Jew. It was God's name for Himself. By using that phrase in the way He did, Jesus was saying as clearly as He possibly could: "I am divine. I am the same one who spoke to Moses on the mountain. I AM God who stands before you." That is why they wanted to kill Him. They didn't want to kill Him for feeding people, or for healing people, or for comforting broken people. They wanted to kill Him because at every turn He rubbed their noses in His claim to have equality with God.

That claim to divine status and honor started very early in His ministry. Mark 2 is nearly as blatant as John 8. In that event Jesus tells a paralytic that his sins are forgiven. The religious leaders are shocked and murmur among themselves that no one can forgive sins except God. Jesus, perceiving what they are only thinking in their hearts, shows them that He is God and can forgive sins, and the proof that He has forgiven this particular man's sins is that He then heals the man of his paralytic condition.

When confronted with the paralytic in Mark 2, Jesus used the common theology of the religious leaders of the day to prove His divinity. He asked if it was easier to say, "Your sins are forgiven," or to say, "Rise, get up, you are healed"? Then comes the dramatic part:

> *" 'But that you may know that the Son of Man has authority on earth to forgive sins'—he said to the paralytic—'I say to you, rise, pick up your bed, and go home.' And he rose and immediately picked up his bed and went out before them all, so that they were all amazed and glorified God, saying, 'We never saw anything like this!' "* (Mark 2:10-12).

By combining the healing with the statement of forgiveness, Jesus is staking His claim to be able to act with an authority that is understood to be reserved for God and God alone. Jesus does not argue with the religious leaders to convince them that their idea of forgiveness is wrong. Rather, He accepts that forgiveness is in God's domain. In the case of this paralytic, forgiveness is God's prerogative and God's alone. What Jesus does by forgiving the man is demonstrate that He, Jesus, has that authority. He can forgive sins. The proof is in the healing of the paralytic following the statement of forgiveness. The man gets up and walks out.

The miracle proves Jesus' power and authority. He is claiming a divine prerogative. The Pharisees know exactly what He is claiming. To their way of thinking Jesus is guilty of blasphemy. They are now looking for reasons to arrest Him and kill Him. A short time later, in Mark 3:6, when Jesus performs another miracle—this time healing on the Sabbath—they decide He must die. Jesus is doing things and saying things that only God is allowed to do and say. For that blasphemy they begin to plot His demise.

Jesus also made provocative statements regarding His equality with the Father, out of the hearing of the public, when He was with His followers. On the last night of His life Jesus wanted His disciples to understand what the future would hold, and that they not fear the future because he had seen the Father:

> *"Jesus said to him, 'Have I been with you so long, and you*

still do not know me, Philip? Whoever has seen me has seen the Father. How can you say, "Show us the Father"? Do you not believe that I am in the Father and the Father is in me? The words that I say to you I do not speak on my own authority, but the Father who dwells in me does his works. Believe me that I am in the Father and the Father is in me, or else believe on account of the works themselves.'" (John 14:9-11).

Here once again Jesus is claiming equality with God that cannot be mistaken for anything else. There is such an identity between Jesus and God the Father that to see one is to see the other. There is such a connection between Father and Son, such an equality that one is in the other and vice versa. It is what allows Jesus to say so boldly that He and the Father are one.

In addition to Jesus' own understanding found in the Gospels, the rest of the New Testament is crystal clear that He is God in the flesh as well. Consider just a few of the more obvious statements:

"For in him the whole fullness of deity dwells bodily" (Colossians 2:9).

"In the beginning was the Word, and the Word was with God, and the Word was God" (John 1:1).

"But in these last days he has spoken to us by his Son, whom he appointed the heir of all things, through whom also he created the world. He is the radiance of the glory of God and the exact imprint of his nature" (Hebrews 1:2-3a).

OK, so what? Jesus claimed to be God and the rest of the New Testament agrees with Him. What difference does that make for you and me? The "so what" is that you have to do something with Jesus and who He claimed to be. You really cannot just let that claim hang out there as if it doesn't matter to you or your life. The reason is this: If Jesus' claim to deity is true, then how you respond to it is the most important step you will ever take. C.S. Lewis popularized the dilemma and the choices with his "Lord, liar, lunatic" options.

It goes like this. Jesus claimed to be God. His claim is either true or it is not. If is not true, then He either knew it was not true and thus He was a liar, or He thought it was true and thus He was a lunatic nutjob with a divinity complex. The other option is that it is true that He is God, the Lord, and as such we must devote ourselves to following Him, wherever He leads and no matter what. The command that He gave His followers right before He left them, in Matthew 28:18-19, was that they were to make disciples, followers of Jesus who would obey everything He commanded. That is the implication for us. Jesus claimed to be the Lord and demonstrated that He is. We are then called to follow, love, and obey Him with everything we have and everything we are.

There is little in the way of biblical truth that is more radical, in the sense of being at the root or core of what we must believe, than the doctrine of Jesus being fully God and fully man. This truth is also among the most provocative. It gets Muslims in a rage, causes Jews to shake their heads in befuddlement, leads Hindus to argue that Jesus is just one of many gods, and causes countless nominal Christians around the world to pull back into a theological shell and ignore the implications and complexities.

Jesus being fully God and fully man is at the heart of our salvation. If He is just a man, then His death on the cross is an insignificant blip in history, hardly worth mentioning. If He is not God, then He was just some shyster of a religious teacher and charlatan who ran afoul of the authorities. Or He truly was a nutjob who thought He was divine. Either way, His death can in no way be beneficial to us. Not as an example, and certainly not as an atonement for sin. If Jesus was not God in the flesh, then we still have our sin and guilt hanging over us.

CHAPTER 5

IS JESUS REALLY THE ONLY WAY TO HEAVEN?

"Jesus said to him, 'I am the way, and the truth, and the life. No one comes to the Father except through me.'" — John 14:6

"'Let it be known to all of you and to all the people of Israel that by the name of Jesus Christ of Nazareth, whom you crucified, whom God raised from the dead—by him this man is standing before you well. This Jesus is the stone that was rejected by you, the builders, which has become the cornerstone. And there is salvation in no one else, for there is no other name under heaven given among men by which we must be saved.'" —Acts 4:10-12

"Jesus can't possibly be the only way to heaven." — Oprah Winfrey

WANT TO START A religious argument that could easily lead to an all-out fight? Make the claim that faith in Jesus is the only way to heaven. You will quickly find yourself on the receiving end of numerous accusations of your narrow-mindedness, your religious snobbery, your unenlightened bigotry—as if there is such a thing as enlightened bigotry—and your holier-than-thou, judgmental self-righteousness. In post-modern Western culture we are repulsed by anyone claiming that their way is the only right way. We refuse to be boxed in and limited. Rather, we love having options. We hate being restricted.

It seems to be part of the DNA of Western cultures that we don't want to be told that we can't have something and we don't want to be told that there is only one way to do something. We are always looking for exceptions to the rule and wanting to be catered to according to our personal likes and desires. When I was a teenager and we went to McDonald's after ice skating on a Friday night it was easy to decide what you would order. The options were limited: hamburger, cheeseburger, Big Mac, or filet of fish. It was a big deal when the Quarter Pounder was added. Now the choices seem endless. And places like Burger King let you know you can have it your way, not just one of the myriad of predetermined ways other places offer you. Of course, the height of our option-loving culture has got to be when someone orders their "double-tall, soy, caramel-mocha, extra-shot, chai, no-fat latte, with room for cream," or whatever it is that they have made up as their required, personalized, get-them-going morning beverage.

This love for options has carried over into our religious convictions. More and more people are selecting from a smorgasbord of religious ideas and customizing their faith. Take a little "love your neighbor" from Jesus. Add a side of meditation from Buddha, a dash of vegan from Hinduism, and a little Kabbalah from Judaism, and you have your own religion. Everyone should have their own religion and find their own path to God, or the afterlife, or whatever goal they have in mind.

Interestingly, there is not even agreement on where we are all trying to go on these paths of our own choosing. If we can't agree on the destination, far be it from anyone to claim that their path is the only path or even the best one. And never, ever insinuate that someone else is on the wrong path or made the wrong choice. It all reminds me of Alice in Wonderland, when she asks if she is going the right way. When asked where it is she is trying to go she doesn't really know. The reply is, "Then I suppose any road will do." If you don't know if you are wanting to go to Heaven, Nirvana, Valhalla, or Hell, then I suppose any road will do.

In an era that promotes tolerance as the highest of virtues, along with the idea that truth is relative, the end result is that no one can tell you your ideas are wrong. On the other side of the coin, it is considered outrageous to claim that Jesus is the one and only, exclusive way for people to go to heaven. It might be one thing to say that a particularly rare and eccentric religious idea is wrong. For instance, you might be able to get away with saying that worshiping Basset Hounds as the supreme being is just strange, or that sitting inside a glass pyramid in your backyard for three hours a day in order to absorb positive energy is a waste of time—although I suspect that for growing numbers of people those are just as acceptable as anything else. Still, it is another thing altogether to claim that every religious idea in the world but yours is wrong. We just don't like the notion that one way is the only way and all other ways are false. I have even noticed that MapQuest now gives you multiple routes to choose from. It used to be that when you asked for directions you got the quickest, most direct route. You wanted to get from point A to point B and you expected to be told the most direct, hassle-free way. Not any more. Now you get to pick. Do you want the quickest, second-quickest, or the long circuitous route? Do you want it with toll roads or without? Do you want scenic and leisurely or sterile and quick?

When it comes to the exclusive claims of Christianity about Jesus, I have heard it more often than I can count: "What about all the people in the world who don't believe in Jesus, who follow Buddha or Confucius or some other teacher? How can you say that they won't go to heaven?"

Well, there are a couple of reasons why I think we must say that. First and foremost among them is what Jesus said in John 14:6, *"I am the way, and the truth, and the life. No one comes to the Father except through me."*

Jesus made it very clear that the way to the Father, and ultimately the way to eternal life in heaven, is through a relationship of faith in Him. The rest of the New Testament affirms this over and over again. There could be nothing more clear in this regard than what Peter says on the Day of Pentecost, just weeks after the crucifixion and resurrection of Jesus. Speaking of Jesus he says:

"And there is salvation in no one else, for there is no other name under heaven given among men by which we must be saved" (Acts 4:12).

I have heard average churchgoers, elders, pastors, and even the occasional bishop state that there must be more ways to heaven than just Jesus. One Anglican bishop said that to limit salvation to only those who come to God through Jesus would be to limit God, and she just could not possibly think that we should be limiting God that way. Never mind the fact that if God has chosen to limit Himself in this way, that we dare not remove those self-imposed limits as if to say that we know better than God. You see, the good bishop hasn't realized her sword can cut both ways.

The only way she, or anyone else, can hold to such a position and say that there are other ways to eternal life is to completely discount everything that the Bible teaches on the subject. That means you must completely discount what God Himself has said about Himself. We do not limit God when we say that the only way to heaven is through Jesus. God has set that limit. God, in His Word, has said that to be certain of a place in eternity with God you must trust Jesus Christ as your Lord and Savior. You must believe that He died and rose again in order to pay the penalty for your sins and conquer death on your behalf.

Is that provocative? You bet—to the point that it gets folks riled up and upset. It says that some people are wrong; some people may not get to heaven. Some people may be left out because they do not know and trust Jesus. I will be honest, I wish it was otherwise. I wish I could stand up with conviction and say to the whole world: "It doesn't matter who or what you believe in. We are all on a path of our own choosing, and eventually all those paths will lead to God and heaven, so carry on and just be sincere." I would love to be able to say that. It would be so much easier, so much more peaceful and conflict-free. I could mind my own business and never again get into a debate with someone who thought I was narrow-minded and bigoted because I take Jesus at His word. But I can't. I just can't discount the words of the Bible no matter how uncomfortable they make me or how much pushback they provoke from other people.

Of course there are certainly some folks who would discount the Bible altogether. For them it only makes sense that if you are sincere in what you believe, then you will live forever. The thought is that sincerity, not truth, is the higher of the two virtues. The supreme being who many believe is out there somewhere is thought of as one who is only gracious and compassionate and would never, ever draw a line in the sand. This only-gracious, only-compassionate, only-loving God would never make right and wrong, truth and falsehood so important as to determine someone's eternal destiny. So surely with such a God, the good, sincere Buddhist, or sincere follower of Confucianism, or committed Taoist, or devoted Hindu, or even the dedicated Islamic Jihadist, will still go to heaven?

ALL HEAVENS ARE NOT CREATED EQUAL

The question is, "Is Jesus the only way to heaven?" In answering that, most people only focus on the "path." Is it just Jesus or are other options just as good? But there really are two critical parts of the question. The first is the nature of the path. Second is the nature of the destination. So many people want to say that all paths lead to God and heaven, and they affirm the variety of paths. But do we all have the same idea about where the paths lead? Will the Buddhist who is on a path to what she thinks is Nirvana be suddenly stunned, or even disappointed, when she dies and arrives in, say, Islam's Paradise? Will the Hindu be stunned when, upon death and his final time of reincarnation, he is finally released from this life, to find Abraham and Moses welcoming him into heaven? Will the Christian be miffed at being welcomed into heaven by Vishnu?

The problem here is the limited understanding that most Westerners with quasi-Christian backgrounds have when it comes to other religions. Liberal Christians and secular thinkers often project their understanding of God and heaven onto other religions and simply assume that those other religious people want to get to the same supreme being and eternal bliss that they do. Far from it! Buddhists and Taoists are not looking for any god and not looking for existence in an eternal paradise. Not only are they on different paths but they are intentionally headed for a different destination—that is why they are on a different path.

Major misconceptions about heaven and the afterlife have led to huge errors when it comes to what people think heaven is like. When we consider the question of heaven and what happens when we die we need to understand that the Bible speaks of a two-stage process. When a follower of Jesus dies, the body ceases to function but the person lives on as a spirit. Right now, as you read this, there is a host of people who have died trusting Christ and they are gathered around the throne of God, worshiping Him. When Jesus was on the cross He promised one thief, "This day you shall be with me in paradise." At death that man found himself in a spiritual paradise with Jesus, even though both their bodies were still hanging on crosses.

But this current spiritual state is not what eternity will be. The Bible tells us that the ultimate goal God has for creation is that it will be redeemed, restored, made new again like at the beginning, before Adam and Eve sinned. In 1 Corinthians 15, Paul talks about the resurrection that will come at the end of the age. The bodies of the dead will be resurrected and re-united with their spirits. Those bodies will be changed in some way so that Paul calls them "glorified bodies":

"I tell you this, brothers: flesh and blood cannot inherit the kingdom of God, nor does the perishable inherit the imperishable. Behold! I tell you a mystery. We shall not all sleep, but we shall all be changed, in a moment, in the twinkling of an eye, at the last trumpet. For the trumpet will sound, and the dead will be raised imperishable, and we shall be changed. For this perishable body must put on the imperishable, and this mortal body must put on immortality" (1 Corinthians 15:50-53).

Those bodies that have been reunited with their spirits and made imperishable will inhabit the redeemed creation in which heaven and earth become one. British author and bishop N.T. Wright has done a masterful job of explaining this biblical truth in his book, *Surprised by Hope.*

When we look at other religions we find that, in many cases, they don't even want to go to heaven. The Buddhist doctrine is that all of life is suffering and the goal is to end all suffering. That goal is something called Nirvana. It is a state of being absorbed, if you will, into the great nothingness of the cosmos. You no longer have an individual existence or awareness of yourself. The Buddhist longs for an existence in which physical reality is no longer a factor. Redeeming creation into an eternal reconciliation with heaven is out of the question. For the Buddhist, the Christian idea of heaven and earth becoming one, and living forever in that state, would be seen as a step backwards. There is no concept of redemption, either for the individual or for creation. The Hindu faces a similar though slightly different path. For him, the cycle of death and reincarnation presents life as a giant wheel. The cycle or wheel of time goes around and around every time you die and are reincarnated. The goal is to stop coming back, to stop the wheel of time from turning, and to become one with creation. It is another loss of self and identity. It is not going to heaven, but being released from this physical reality that is the goal of the Hindu. Clearly, these various religions are on different paths because they are trying to get somewhere different from the paradise that Jesus promised the thief next to Him.

WESTERN EMBARRASSMENT OVER THE EXCLUSIVE JESUS

For the most part, it is only people raised in a Western philosophical mindset who have a problem with the exclusivity of Jesus. It is only people raised in some sort of "Christian" culture who seem to be embarrassed by the claim of Jesus to be the only way to heaven. Adherents to other religious systems don't seem to have this problem. The average Hindu has no problem saying the Muslims are on the wrong path and need to become Hindus. The average Buddhist has no problem saying that the Hindu needs to give it up and start following the path of Buddha. But here is the truly ironic part of this discussion: Christians, supposed followers of Jesus, are the ones who are embarrassed by the claims of exclusivity of salvation in Christ alone. And here is the truly bizarre part of this: even though other religions are comfortable with their own exclusivity, Hindus saying Muslims must become Hindus and vice-versa, most other religions, rather than rejecting Jesus and requiring others to reject Him, actually try to incorporate Him into their faith in some way. Muslims call Him an honored prophet and believe He was born of a virgin. He is second only to Mohammed in terms of being revered. Buddhists refer to Jesus as a Bodhisattva, or an enlightened one who shows the path to others. Hindus think of Him as an incarnation of Vishnu, one of their highest gods.

When I first realized that so many other religions wanted a piece of Jesus it made me think of the first chapter of Paul's letter to the Romans. In it he points out that God has placed within every human being a knowledge of the truth, but that we have suppressed that truth under the falsehood of our own made-up religions. But like anything that we suppress, that truth will make itself known in unexpected ways. As a result, even in religious systems that are opposed to what the Bible teaches, there is a need to honor Jesus. Somehow the One who claimed to be the only way finds expression in religions that would otherwise deny Him. No other religious figure from history is treated this way. Muslims have no place for Buddha. Hindus want nothing to do with Mohammed. Buddhists rejected Vishnu and all other Hindu gods long ago. Yet they all seem to have this need to hedge their bets and keep Jesus close by.

There is no need for a follower of Jesus to be embarrassed by the exclusive claims of Jesus. If other religions want a part of Jesus, why shouldn't His followers be willing to push further and say that with Jesus it is all or nothing? He is the Lord who rightly demands our allegiance. Our highest command is to love Him with all our heart, mind, soul, and strength. It is Jesus who is the way to eternal life.

THE FATHER'S HOUSE HAS MANY ROOMS

On the last night of His life, before going to the cross, Jesus was trying to comfort His followers in the face of His coming death. In John 14:1-2 He says, *"Let not your hearts be troubled. Believe in God; believe also in me. In my Father's house are many rooms. If it were not so, would I have told you that I go to prepare a place for you?"* It is fascinating that people who are quick to discount so many other parts of the Bible will latch onto these words about many rooms. I have heard people claim time and again that Jesus' speaking of many rooms is an affirmation of the validity of other religions. It is a variation on the idea that there are many roads to the top of the mountain, but in this case there are many rooms, many religious systems that get you into God's house. People claim that these words of Jesus are an affirmation of there being many ways to heaven and a statement against the exclusivity of Jesus for salvation.

It never ceases to amaze me that people can be so blind to what a text says. This is no exception. Just look at the context. Jesus does not want to comfort His disciples by letting them know that there are many paths to heaven. That is a modern Western model. We want to be comforted by knowing that there are numerous possibilities and our odds of hitting one of those options are increased. Rather, Jesus is comforting them by letting them know that He is the only way to heaven. The comfort comes in the knowledge that they can rest assured because He is going there to make a place for them.

In verse 6 Jesus says, *"I am the way, the truth, and the life. No one comes to the Father except through me."* There is only one way to heaven, through faith in Jesus, though there are many rooms in heaven, in God's house. There is no need to worry because Jesus is preparing a room for you. You can rest assured. Your reservation is secured. Your room will not be given to someone else, because Jesus has prepared it. The comfort comes in the promise of Jesus that He is the only way to heaven and that He will make sure you have a place.

The first disciples took comfort in the simplicity of what Jesus was saying. They took comfort in it because it was Jesus who was saying it. They knew they had a room because Jesus promised it. They trusted Him and His word. That is the essence of faith and a relationship with Jesus. It is about trust. Believing in Jesus is all about trusting Him, trusting Him as the only way to the Father.

CHAPTER 6

THE SCANDAL OF THE CROSS

"The notion that God would require a bloody sacrifice on a cross in order to forgive sins is barbaric." — anonymous seminary professor

"For the word of the cross is folly to those who are perishing, but to us who are being saved it is the power of God. For it is written, 'I will destroy the wisdom of the wise, and the discernment of the discerning I will thwart.' "
— 1 Corinthians 1:18-19

"... knowing that you were ransomed from the futile ways inherited from your forefathers, not with perishable things such as silver or gold, but with the precious blood of Christ, like that of a lamb without blemish or spot."
— 1 Peter 1:18-19

"The longer I dwell on the Cross in my thoughts, the more I am satisfied that there is more to learn at the foot of the Cross than anywhere else in the world." — J. C. Ryle

THERE HAVE BEEN COUNTLESS hymns and songs written about the cross. Innumerable paintings and sculptures depict Jesus in His final moments, suffering the agony of the cross. On one level there is a fascination with the cross. But on another level there is a certain bewilderment, confusion, even disdain about the cross and its meaning. What lies at the heart of this fascination and disdain is the extremely provocative notion that God required the death of Jesus on the cross in order to wipe away the penalty of human sin.

I once heard from a rather theologically liberal seminary professor that the idea that God would require a sacrifice in blood in order to forgive people is brutal and barbaric. To think that God actually planned for and desired the crucifixion just doesn't fit the idea of God that many people have. It certainly did not fit that professor's idea. It was clear from his lectures that he viewed God more as a kind being who wanted people to experience enlightenment than as the God of the Bible who was both loving and just and dealt with sin. To him and many others, the requirement of a sacrifice is the stuff of archaic, ancient superstition. It is certainly not the stuff of modern, post-Enlightenment, civilized and sophisticated people. Yet, shockingly, the Bible speaks in clear sacrificial terms about the cross and even acknowledges that to pre-modern, pre-Enlightenment Greeks and Jews the cross was abhorrent.

During the 1960s there was a social revolution going on in America. Part of that revolution involved rejection of authority and viewed government as oppressive and brutal, only wanting to keep power and hold people in bondage. Social revolution was in the air and on the nightly news. Jesus was viewed as the ultimate social revolutionary. People said He went to the cross because the governing religious leaders and the Romans were trying to hold on to power and needed Him out of the way. That way of thinking allowed people like my seminary professor to excuse God from any part in the crucifixion. He could conclude that the cross was not in God's plan. It was not a necessary act, required for the forgiveness of sin. Rather, in his view, the crucifixion of Jesus was the result of evil political and religious systems. Interestingly, he would also have wanted to deny human sin: there was no need for a sacrifice on the cross because people are basically good in his world. It is only systems, structures, impersonal entities that are evil. So his view of God as a benign and benevolent being who only loves in sweet, wonderful ways could remain intact only if the cross, rather than being God's plan to turn away His wrath, was simply a tragedy of social and political power run amuck.

Nothing could be further from the truth. Jesus made it perfectly clear that He came into the world in order to give His life as a bloody sacrifice and ransom for sinners. How else do you understand what He meant when He rebuked His followers as they jockeyed for position to see which of them would be the greatest?

"But Jesus called them to him and said, 'You know that the rulers of the Gentiles lord it over them, and their great ones exercise authority over them. It shall not be so among you. But whoever would be great among you must be your servant, and whoever would be first among you must be your slave, even as the Son of Man came not to be served but to serve, and to give his life as a ransom for many' " (Matthew 20:25-28).

Jesus came into the world for the express purpose of going to the cross and being a sacrifice in order to atone for the sins of many. The scandal of God coming in the flesh is hard enough for people to accept. That this God would submit Himself to an horrific death by crucifixion is even harder to take. It is difficult for us to accept, and it was even harder for His close friends to accept.

Jesus asked His disciples what the buzz was among the crowds of people following Him. Who did they think Jesus was? As the disciples gave an account of the various ideas, ranging from Elijah to John the Baptist come back to life, Jesus asked who they, the disciples, thought He was. Peter correctly answered that Jesus was the Christ, the Son of the Living God (Matthew 16:13-20). Jesus praised Peter and said that the Father had revealed that truth to him, and with His identity as Messiah affirmed Jesus began to teach that He must now head to Jerusalem and be arrested, beaten, and made to suffer and die. He didn't say anything about crucifixion in particular, but Peter reacted vehemently by pulling

Jesus aside and "correcting" Him. Peter couldn't stand this idea of Jesus facing death; it was out of the question that the Messiah should suffer the indignity of being arrested, beaten, and killed.

It was scandalous enough to them that Jesus said He would be arrested, beaten, and killed. One can only imagine how freaked out Peter and the other disciples would have been if Jesus told them about being crucified. Why? Because crucifixion in the first century was about more than just being put to death. It was more than just a physically hideous way to die. It was also a scandalous way to die. Roman citizens were generally spared crucifixion because it was considered to be too demeaning. It was most often used for slaves and the most heinous of criminals. It wasn't just that you were executed, it was what the manner of execution said about the person. To be crucified meant that you were among the lowest of the low, the dregs of society. It was his Roman citizenship that spared the Apostle Paul from death on a cross, being quickly beheaded instead. It was Peter's lack of Roman citizenship that resulted in him being nailed to a cross—upside down, at his request, because he thought he was unworthy to die the same way Jesus had.

It was the nature of Christ's death as one being crucified that was such a stumbling block to both Jews and Greeks who heard the gospel in the first century. Paul puts it this way in 1 Corinthians 1:23: *"But we preach Christ crucified, a stumbling block to Jews and folly to Gentiles."* For Jews who were looking for a powerful messianic deliverer in the mold of David, it was impossible to get their minds around a crucified Jesus being Messiah. For the Greek mindset, so focused on honor, strength, and power, it was laughable to think that a shamed criminal, crucified in Judea, could be the hope of the world. It was this scandalous nature of the cross that forced early Christian apologists to spend so much of their time defending the cross. The Greek mindset was to reject a crucified messiah as absurd. A messiah would be a man of power and honor, not one suffering the indignity of crucifixion. As an aside, Muslims also deny that Jesus was crucified on the grounds that Allah would never allow the second-greatest prophet to suffer such indignity. As counterintuitive as it may be, the biblical message is that to accept the scandalous cross is our only hope.

REJECTING THE CROSS FOR A LOVING GOD

We don't have the same cultural issues with the cross that the Jews or Greeks had during the New Testament era. What we have is rather more sophisticated and personal reasons for being scandalized by it. The seminary professor who rejects the possibility of a "bloody sacrifice" for the forgiveness of sins is not someone who rejects the cross because he is looking for a messiah in the mold of David. He is not rejecting the cross because he has a Greek view of honor or strength. Instead he is rejecting the sacrificial death of Christ on two related grounds, the inability to see God as being one who must deal harshly with sin, and the unwillingness to see himself as being in need of such a sacrifice for his own sins.

If there is anything we have come to believe about God in Western culture it is that God is love, all love, and nothing but love. We cannot possibly conceive of such a loving God being harsh or demanding or in any way in need of a sacrifice to assuage His wrath and wash away our guilt. Our loving God has become one who we expect to simply give us a free pass and welcome us into heaven no matter what we do or say. Love trumps everything. Or as Rob Bell has recently said with the title of his book, *Love Wins*.

Without a doubt love is one of the more important and evident character traits of God. The case could certainly be made that in the past Christians have been negligent in understanding, teaching, and modeling God's loving character. But the remedy to that imbalance is not to swing completely in the other direction and treat love as if it is God's only character trait. Our loving God is still holy, just, righteous, jealous, and sometimes angry and wrathful. Any attempt to ignore those, or any other, character traits results in a blatantly false picture of God and is in fact a base form of idolatry. It is a false image of God and leads to a distorted understanding and warped relationship with Him.

One of the aspects of ministry that I love at Northland Church, where I serve as one of the pastors, is that worship always focuses on an attribute of God. Worship is not built around the latest cool idea for a sermon series. Certainly worship and the sermon are thematically connected, but they connect via a particular attribute of God. So on any given weekend people will be reminded that we worship God for who He is and what He has done. One week we may be worshiping God as a God of love, the next maybe a God of holiness, then power, righteousness, jealousy, compassion, wisdom, and so on. What this approach has served to do over the years is help people have a more complete view of our amazing God and not fall into the trap of viewing Him only through the lens of our own desire. Sadly, many people have a very stunted and distorted view of God. Their view of Him as only loving, kind, and benevolent is false and warped. As is, by the way, the opposite view of God as only vengeful, angry, and judgmental.

Related to this false and warped view of God as only loving and kind is our false and warped view of ourselves. The cross is scandalous to the twenty-first-century mind because it brutally depicts the fate that we deserve because of our sin and we just don't want to admit that we sin, or that our sin is really a big deal. As I said in chapter two, we are not OK. Try as we might to cover over and ignore our sin and its subsequent guilt, we cannot escape it. The image of a battered and bloody Jesus, gasping His last breath on a cross while begging forgiveness for the very people who nailed Him there, is both shocking and scandalous. And it is only understandable in light of our sin. But it is in part the reality of our sin, and the desire to deny it and avoid dealing with it, that makes the cross so repulsive to us. We are embarrassed and ashamed that the cross was only necessary because we rejected a loving and merciful God and forced His hand of justice into action. The cross is a stumbling block because in it we are forced to come face to face with our own ugliness, our own evil, our own sinfulness.

Only when we are willing to accept the reality and seriousness of our sin, in light of all God's character traits, or attributes, are we able to fully appreciate and even embrace the cross. It is in the cross that we find not a stumbling block and foolishness but the only real answer to our sin and guilt in the face of a just and loving God. It is on the cross that we see the depth of God's love, *"for God so loved the world that he gave his only son"* (John 3:16). It is also on the cross that we see God's justice and wrath dealing with our sin:

> *"Surely he has borne our griefs and carried our sorrows; yet we esteemed him stricken, smitten by God, and afflicted. But he was pierced for our transgressions; he was crushed for our iniquities; upon him was the chastisement that brought us peace"* (Isaiah 53:4-5).

We are sinners. We are guilty. Sending Jesus into the world for the express purpose of giving His life as a bloody sacrifice on the cross is how a just and loving God's deals with that sin. Post-Enlightenment man and woman may recoil at that truth, but we do so to our own demise. Embracing that truth is the only way to really make sense of the cross. Jesus as the misguided social revolutionary who was caught in corrupt political machinery is woefully lacking as an explanation for the cross. Jesus the mystic, who by His death becomes an example for us of the virtues of sacrifice, is even more bankrupt. In that scenario what was He sacrificing for and what does it have to do with us? If the cross didn't actually accomplish some benefit for people, then the death of Christ was simply a tragedy. When you sacrifice for someone there should be some benefit to that person. Saying that Jesus' death is an example of sacrifice for others without having some objective benefit to others just doesn't make any sense.

THE MANY-FACETED GLORY OF THE CROSS

In Western Christianity the major doctrinal focus when people talk about the cross and atonement has been what I call their judicial aspects. God is a just God who must punish sin. We deserve to be punished for our sin and that punishment would eventually mean spending an eternity in hell, separated from God's love and grace. But because God is also loving and merciful, He sent Jesus into the world as the second Adam. He lived a sinless life and therefore had no guilt of His own and was free from the punishment for sin. Out of His love for us He went to the cross and offered Himself in our place. Jesus paid the penalty for our sin. So both the justice of God and the mercy of God are satisfied.

A very popular illustration is that of God being a judge who pronounces a penalty for our sin. It is a penalty we are unable to pay, so God the judge, who also happens to be our Father, gets down from His judge's bench, stands next to us, and pays the fine on our behalf. So justice is served because the just penalty for sin has been paid. But mercy is also served because God pays our penalty.

This judicial idea of the cross is a long-held, biblical perspective and used often in Western evangelism. But it is not the only biblical perspective. Like a diamond with many facets, the cross becomes more glorious in our eyes the more we become aware of its numerous facets.

On a recent church-planting trip to Western Zambia I saw this in real life. We had a team living in the bush for a week, visiting small villages, sharing the story of Jesus, and starting a few churches. At one point people were hearing the explanation of the cross and its benefits, in the traditional Western, judicial illustration. The looks on the faces of the people were of complete incomprehension; this idea of a judge and penalty for sin, the payment of the penalty by the judge, simply had no cultural connection for them.

But there was a facet of the cross that connected very closely with their culture. It has to do with curses. In the Zambian culture all of life is lived in the reality of curses. Nearly all decisions are made in light of the potential of curses. People will not expand the size of their farm out of fear that a neighbor will get jealous over their growing wealth and go to a witch doctor and have a curse placed on them and their expanded farm. People live in fear that if someone is angry with them, that person may place a death curse on them. Ancestors are worshiped out of fear that if they are not honored, their spirits will return and curse the living members of the family. No one is happy with the practical implications of this worldview—except the witch doctors, who do a booming business, being paid in chickens, cows, and goats to place and remove curses, sometimes accepting payment in the morning to place a curse and then in the evening taking payment from the cursed person to remove it.

The Apostle Paul makes the connection between the cross and the removal of curses. *"Christ redeemed us from the curse of the law by becoming a curse for us—for it is written, Cursed is everyone who hangs on a tree"* (Galatians 3:13). The point Paul is making is that we are helpless because of the negative spiritual impact of our sin. The law of God relentlessly makes us aware of the deadly impact of our sin. We are cursed. Jesus' death on the cross removes the curse of the law and the death that comes with our sin.

As soon as the Zambians heard that Jesus died to remove all their curses and remove the impact of them, they immediately wanted to know more about Jesus. They wanted the freedom from the curse that comes only because of Christ and the cross. They saw another facet of the cross that the typical Westerner doesn't see or appreciate. In fact, if you preached an evangelistic sermon in America or Europe and started talking about following Jesus so you can be free from curses, most folks would look at you like you just had just grown a third eye on your forehead. But the cross is so rich and full in its glory and implications that, no matter the culture or background of a person, there is something about it that will speak to them.

The cross, as hard as it may be to embrace, was God's way of opening the door to a relationship with Him. It was God's way of both expressing His love and satisfying His justice. Did the political machinery have a role in bringing about the crucifixion of Jesus? Of course it did. Was the self-sacrifice demonstrated on the cross by Jesus a great example for us to follow? Of course. But it is more, much more. It is the heart of the gospel, and the glorious way in which God has demonstrated both His just and loving natures.

Chapter 7

TAKE UP YOUR CROSS AND FOLLOW ME

"Not only that, but we rejoice in our sufferings, knowing that suffering produces endurance, and endurance produces character, and character produces hope, and hope does not put us to shame, because God's love has been poured into our hearts through the Holy Spirit who has been given to us."
— Romans 5:3-5

"And whoever does not take his cross and follow me is not worthy of me."
— Matthew 10:38

"Jesus calls a man and bids him to come and die." — Dietrich Bonhoeffer

AS SCANDALOUS AS THE idea of a messiah dying on a cross may be, the followers of Jesus had to be equally shocked, if not more so, by His call to them, urging that they too take up their cross and follow Him. For a first-century person living in the Roman Empire, few things could have been more perplexing, revolting, and scandalous. To be told that you should willingly prepare for your own death by crucifixion was like asking someone to register as a sex offender even though they had never done anything remotely like that. It was asking a person to voluntarily die in a most horrendous way reserved only for the most shameful of people.

But that is just what Jesus asks, that we be willing to go to our own crucifixion and carry our cross as a sign of that willingness to die.

One of my favorite books of all time is *Band of Brothers* by Stephen Ambrose. It was turned into an award-winning mini-series on HBO. The story follows Easy Company of the 506th Battalion of the 101st Airborne division from their time in training in Georgia, to D-Day in Normandy, all the way to the capture of Hitler's mountain retreat, The Eagle's Nest. One of the threads in this true story follows a young private by the name of Albert Blithe. Following D-Day he is clearly shaken by the death and destruction that is all around him. He becomes very tentative and uncertain. He is understandably dealing with the fear of death. A somewhat cold and hardened lieutenant by the name of Spears tells Blithe what his problem is. He looks him straight in the eye and says, "You don't know that you're already dead. Once you accept the fact that you are a dead man, there is nothing to fear." The private considers those words and eventually comes to grips with that reality, beginning to do his job as a soldier with a confidence that can only come from having nothing left to lose.

Dietrich Bonhoeffer was also in Europe during World War II. A pastor in Germany who opposed Hitler, he was eventually arrested. His execution was personally ordered by Hitler, just a month before the end of the war. Prior to his death, Bonhoeffer is quoted as saying that Jesus "bids us to come and die." Like Blithe, Bonhoeffer learned an important lesson. It is found in the words of Jesus, in Matthew 16:24-26:

> *"Then Jesus told his disciples, 'If anyone would come after me, let him deny himself and take up his cross and follow me. For whoever would save his life will lose it, but whoever loses his life for my sake will find it. For what will it profit a man if he gains the whole world and forfeits his soul? Or what shall a man give in return for his soul?' "*

So much of what we do in life seems designed to protect our lives or enhance them in some way. I am speaking not just of our physical lives, though that is true enough. I am speaking of our lives even in the less tangible sense of our dreams, hopes, image, comfort, reputation, and pleasures. We spend so much time and effort trying to acquire and hold onto the things that we think make life worth living. Some of those things are tangible: our house, car, corner office, trophies, or relationships. Some of them are less tangible but no less real and alluring. They include things like fame, respect, power, security, or a host of things that are on our "bucket list" that we feel we must do before we die, in order to make life complete.

Jesus makes it shockingly clear that when we try to acquire and protect such things in our life, even our life itself, what we really end up doing is losing our life. We can spend eighty years chasing after such things, but as Solomon said it is chasing after the wind. The way Jesus put it is that we can gain those things and end up losing our soul. In the end we will have neither the life we chased nor the life He offers.

There is, however, another option. That is to consider that we have already died. The life that seeks after all the things of this world must be put to death. The sign of such a death is that we have decided to follow Jesus and have hefted our cross onto our shoulders. In the first century, any man seen carrying a cross was a dead man walking. Like the prisoners on death row in the movie, *The Green Mile,* the follower of Christ has already given up the earthly hopes and dreams of this life and embraced his or her death. The first-century follower of Christ recognized that her life was already forfeit. She was breathing and moving, but she was already dead. Jesus is calling us to carry our cross every day. He wants us to consider this life as dead, to give it up, to release it. It is only in such a posture, that of a follower slumped under the weight of the cross, that we will find the freedom to truly live. In such a position we have nothing to lose.

Private Blithe learned this and it freed him to become the soldier he needed to be. The irony for Blithe is that shortly after embracing the truth that he was already dead, he volunteered to be on point, the lead man on patrol. It was the most dangerous place to be. Blithe was shot and evacuated. His wound seemed fatal, and that was the last any of his comrades saw of him. The book and television mini-series report that Blithe died of his wounds a few days after being hit. His family was rather surprised to learn of this when they saw the series; the reason being that Private Blithe did not die as a result of his wounds in World War II. He actually lived for three more decades. He eventually became Master Sergeant Blithe, twice reenlisting in the army, and making over six hundred parachute jumps. He was awarded a Silver Star, three Bronze Stars, and three Purple Hearts. Today he is buried in Arlington Cemetery. Apparently, once he accepted that he was already dead, Albert Blithe lived more than most people ever hope to.

Dietrich Bonhoeffer knew this and it freed him to serve Jesus no matter what. He opposed Hitler and Nazism from the beginning, part of the underground church that worked hard to follow Jesus even as the Nazis tried to restrict and even kill some of them. In 1938 Bonhoeffer was in America, where friends urged him to stay rather than go back to Germany. But Bonhoeffer knew that he had to return to the people of Germany and serve them, even if he die. He acted on his most famous quote, that Jesus bids a man to come and die. On April 9, 1945, Bonhoeffer was hanged. But in the years between 1938 and then Bonhoeffer had the freedom in Christ to live a life that became a legacy and inspiration for millions. He could only have done that if he had already considered his life forfeit for Jesus.

What are you holding onto? What in your life are you clinging to in fear and desperation? The sooner you are willing to release that and give it up to God, the sooner you will be free to experience life as never before. In some way, by considering ourselves dead we become truly alive in Christ. The angst that hovers over so many people, the backdrop of uncertainty and discomfort over life, death, and the future is torn away when we truly take up our cross and become dead men walking. Jesus said that the grain of wheat only truly comes to life when it first falls to the ground and dies. How ironic that we only truly experience life when we first die to ourselves and take up the cross of Christ.

There is more to taking up your cross than just surrendering your fears and anxieties to Jesus. When it comes to following Jesus it is also about surrendering your hopes, dreams, aspirations, longings, comforts, position, property, pleasures, rights, and privileges for the honor of following Jesus above all else. You see, taking up your cross is a symbolic way of saying that your entire life is under the direction of Jesus and you give up ownership of everything you ever wanted in life.

Jesus said that we are to take up our cross and follow Him. The two things go hand in hand. Taking up your cross is a sign that you are willing to forsake everything in life, to give it up. Sacrifice it, and for all intents and purposes, bury it. But it is not enough to simply say to Jesus that you give up that life you had been living. You must add to that the promise of following Christ, making your life His life. This may be the most important, yet neglected aspect of modern, evangelical Christianity.

In many ways we have made the actual following of Jesus a secondary part of the Christian life, at best. Think about how Christianity is so often presented these days. The call to people to become Christians has been whittled down to little more than an event in which you make an affirmation of sorts and walk away feeling momentarily better about your life. Here is what I mean by that. Huge numbers of preachers and teachers talk about "inviting Jesus into your heart." As a result, countless numbers of people have done just that. They prayed a prayer and accepted Jesus. Or they raised a hand, or stood up, or did any number of other things to indicate that they wanted Jesus in their lives.

They added a little bit of Jesus into their lives. And that is the problem. Jesus did not say to add a little bit of Him into your life in order to tweak it, improve it, or even give it a serious makeover. What He said was, Put your old life to death. It is what Jesus means by the repentance part of coming to Him. It is an acknowledgment that your life was a mess and ultimately you made it that way. The only real way to live is to first die to that life. You must dig a hole and bury it, tell God that you know you messed it up royally and that you are going to carry your cross so that from here on out you are putting your life completely in Jesus' hands.

Chapter 8

WORK OUT YOUR SALVATION

"Therefore, my beloved, as you have always obeyed, so now, not only as in my presence but much more in my absence, work out your own salvation with fear and trembling." — Philippians 2:12

"The darkest places in hell are reserved for those who maintain their neutrality in times of moral crisis." — Dante Alighieri

THE BIBLE IS NOT nearly as complicated as people make it out to be. Yet, I have learned that it is simple enough that the least astute child can understand its depths and deep enough that the most skilled of scholars can never fully grasp its implications. Philippians 2:12-13 comes to mind as so perfectly fitting that reality: "Therefore, my beloved, as you have always obeyed, so now, not only as in my presence but much more in my absence, work out your own salvation with fear and trembling, for it is God who works in you, both to will and to work for his good pleasure."

On numerous occasions I have had people ask me about these verses, wondering if there is a contradiction here. People think that Paul is saying our salvation depends on our good works. They get the fear and trembling part because they usually start trembling when they realize they are not doing a very good job of it. But Paul is not saying that our good works, or being a good person, gets you into heaven. We have already seen that salvation is purely a gift from God, bestowed in grace.

The problem is people usually read verse 12 and forget to read verse 13. The verse divisions are great for finding places in the Bible but terrible as a guide to understanding it. Verses 12 and 13 are a complete sentence. To read verse 12 by itself is to only read one half of the thought. We would never do that with any other piece of literature yet we do it with the Bible all the time. Not a good idea.

What Paul is saying is simply this, "When I was with you, you did a great job of living for Jesus. Keep doing this even though I am not there. Work hard at living out the salvation you have been given by God. Why? Because God is working in you and that should be made evident in the way you live."

Paul is not saying that you are saved by being a good person. He is perfectly clear in many other places that we are saved by God's grace and the faith/trust we have in Jesus Christ. The life we live as followers of Christ does not save us, but it should be a life that is consistent with being a follower of Jesus who is saved by God's grace.

Paul does not say, "Work for your salvation," or, "Work at your salvation," or, "Work toward your salvation." All of those would mean that in some way it is your efforts that gain you admission into eternal life. He says to "work out your salvation." In other words, live it out. Plan out your life, live out your life, work out your life in such a way that your salvation is obvious. Additionally, you need to be so committed to living out the Christ-like life that you are driven to it with an urgency that makes you tremble. This quote from Peter O'Brien in his *New International Greek Testament Commentary on Philippians* gets to the point:

> *"It is an exhortation to common action, urging the Philippians to show forth the graces of Christ in their lives, to make their eternal salvation fruitful in the here and now as they fulfill their responsibilities to one another as well as to non-Christians."*

Why such urgency? Why such desperation to live out your salvation? Paul gives the reason in verse 13: "For God is at work in you." What in incredible statement: "Because God is working in you." The sovereign King of the universe is so interested in you personally that in addition to holding everything in the span of His hand and keeping the stars in their courses through the heavens, God is working in your life for His eternal plan to be made manifest.

Sometimes the best way to understand the meaning of a statement is to try to understand its reverse or opposite. We are told to work out our salvation because God is at work in us. What if the statement was, "Don't bother doing anything to live according to the salvation God has given you, and just live with a nonchalant attitude towards Him and His salvation, and don't do anything to promote your relationship with God." If that is what we did we would not be functioning in a neutral way. By being nonchalant about our salvation and relationship with God we would actually be resisting what God is doing in our lives and therefore working against our salvation rather than because of it. Do we really want to be working against what God is doing in our lives? Do we want to face the consequences of having a nonchalant attitude toward our salvation?

Paul says that with fear and trembling we should be working at this life of salvation. Anything less is not being neutral. It is being opposed to what God is doing in our lives. When we fail to love others in Jesus' name, when we fail to be content with what God has given us, when we long for someone who is not our spouse, when we fail to love God with our entire being, we are not simply ignoring something that God has told us. We are actively opposing God and what He is doing. We are working against the very salvation we have been given as a gift. That should cause us to fear and tremble.

It is like failing to exercise. We view that as passive. We are not actively trying to hurt our body when we don't exercise.

We are just not doing anything to actively help it. I think we often look at our Christian life that way. We are passive in it and think that this is somehow acceptable to God because at least we are not actively opposing God. When it comes to physical exercise, the truth is that by failing to exercise you are actually actively working at getting fatter, weaker, and sicker. You have made a decision to do something that harms you. That something is whatever takes the place of healthy physical activity. The same is true of your spiritual well-being. To fail to live a life that is committed to a radical love for God and neighbor is to actively oppose the work that God is doing in you. Every time I fail to love God with all I have, and my neighbor as myself, I am actively fighting against what God is doing in me as He works to shape me into a more Christ-like follower.

The fact that God has worked in me to grant me grace and faith should motivate me to live for Him with all I am. The fact that God has worked in such a way as to pay the penalty for my sin should cause me to tremble before Him. The recognition that my sin is great but God's love for me is greater should cause me to work at living for Him like nothing else I have ever done in my life. I should do it not to earn salvation, but because I have salvation as a gift from a holy and righteous God who is also gracious and merciful.

CHAPTER 9

JESUS SAID "I NEVER KNEW YOU"

" 'Not everyone who says to me, "Lord, Lord," will enter the kingdom of heaven, but the one who does the will of my Father who is in heaven. On that day many will say to me, "Lord, Lord, did we not prophesy in your name, and cast out demons in your name, and do many mighty works in your name?" And then will I declare to them, "I never knew you; depart from me, you workers of lawlessness." ' " —Matthew 7:21-23

" 'Then he will say to those on his left, "Depart from me, you cursed, into the eternal fire prepared for the devil and his angels. For I was hungry and you gave me no food, I was thirsty and you gave me no drink, I was a stranger and you did not welcome me, naked and you did not clothe me, sick and in prison and you did not visit me." ' " — Matthew 25:41-43

YOU CAN'T READ THE parable of the sheep and the goats in Matthew 25, and the warning to people crying, "Lord, Lord," in Matthew 7, without being just a little bit nervous about your eternal destiny. Here are some people in both passages who are certain that they have a place in heaven reserved just for them. Yet Jesus tells them that they are sadly mistaken. It appears from what Jesus says that the problem lies in the fact that they did not do what they were supposed to do, and thus are not saved.

Now, without a doubt, the Bible teaches that we are saved by faith in Christ and even that is not our own doing but a gift from God. Ephesians 2:8-9 is about as clear on this as possible. Our works do not save us. You have read that numerous times already in this book. It is worth repeating again and again. How wonderful is it that God in His mercy, grace, and love has gifted us with the most undeserved blessing in the history of all time? Yet, there is an incredibly important role that our good works play in relation to our salvation.

In Matthew 25:31-46 Jesus tells of sheep and goats that are separated at the judgment. The sheep are welcomed into eternal life and the goats are sent to eternal punishment. When they ask why one group goes to heaven and one does not they are told that one group, the sheep, visited the sick, fed the hungry, and clothed the naked. As a result, they really did those things for Jesus. The other group, the goats, failed to do so and as a result failed to do so for Jesus.

In Matthew 7 we find this subject dealt with in an even more shocking way. Here Jesus doesn't use the metaphor of sheep and goats. He cuts right to the heart of the issue and says that there are people who will be shocked that they don't get into heaven. They will be fully expecting to get in as they call out, "Lord, Lord." But Jesus says that they will be turned aside when He declares that He never knew them.

The goats of Matthew 25 and the unnamed people of Matthew 7 are essentially the same. They are the folks who will get sent off to outer darkness and destruction when they fully expected to be welcomed by the one they called Lord. How is that possible? How can someone go through their whole life calling Jesus Lord, having a right understanding of who He is, maybe even having gone forward at a Billy Graham crusade or a youth retreat, prayed a prayer to accept Jesus into their heart, been assured that they were now saved, gone to church regularly, maybe even served as an elder or deacon, and lo and behold, they get to heaven and Jesus looks them in the eye and says, "Sorry, don't think we have ever met. I don't know you; away with you to a place of punishment"?

What Jesus says and does in this passage runs so contrary to current, popular, evangelical thought and practice that it is a wonder people are not freaking out over these words when they come across them in their Bibles. You have to be in some kind of huge state of denial or oblivion to not be provoked into some kind of reaction, be it bewilderment, concern, fear, debate, or even anger. Jesus telling a group of people who were certain He was their Lord and that they were going to heaven that He doesn't even know them should cause every follower of Christ to ask, Am I a sheep or a goat? I fear that millions of people who have followed the evangelical, revivalist method of praying a prayer of salvation think that have punched their ticket to heaven and there is nothing left for them to do but wait out this life and then spend eternity with Jesus. I know this passage causes me to regularly do an assessment of my life and relationship with Jesus and ask, Am I a sheep or a goat?

So what are we to make of this? Is Jesus teaching that we are saved by works? Is He saying that we can earn our way to heaven when other parts of the Bible clearly say otherwise? Is He saying that we can lose our salvation if we don't do enough good works? The answer is going to be found in understanding the less clear parts of the Bible in light of the perfectly clear parts. We have to use Scripture to understand Scripture.

We have already seen that salvation is a gift of God and we can do nothing to earn or deserve it. The previous discussion from Philippians 2 about working out your salvation still applies here, as does Ephesians 2, which is crystal clear on the question of how we are saved. Ephesians 2:10 says, "It is by grace that you are saved, through faith, not of works so that no one can boast." In the previous chapter we saw that Paul urges us to "work out," meaning live out to the fullest, the salvation we have in Christ. All of this is to say that the good things we do in life, the service to other people, the sacrifice of ourselves for the less fortunate, the visiting of the sick and prisoner, the feeding the hungry, all our service should be evidence of a living faith. These things should point to the reality of a salvation we already possess, not the efforts to possess a salvation we are trying to earn.

What Jesus is saying about the sheep and the goats and about those who call Him "Lord, Lord" is a graphic and powerful lesson of how easy it is for us to get the relationship between faith and works all wrong. Jesus makes it clear that those who have a real faith in Him, one that is accompanied by a relationship of "knowing" one another, will be people who sacrificially serve the weakest and most downtrodden among us. True saving faith will demonstrate itself by how we live or, more precisely, how we love. If we love God with all we have and all we are, we will love our neighbor. We will serve them and care for them. That is what Jesus says the sheep did. When they served other people they were in reality serving Jesus. They loved the people around them and as a result it was obvious that they loved God too. That kind of faith will save you.

On the other hand, faith that does not show up by loving others is really no faith at all. That kind of faith will not save you. The goats thought they had faith. They thought Jesus was their Lord. But their faith was pure lip service. It was not people service. They talked a good game. They did not walk the talk. What the Bible teaches is that if you have a faith that is guided by loving God and loving your neighbor, then you will show people your faith by how you serve them in their time of need. Those good works do not save you, but they are a critical piece of evidence of the faith that you have that does save you. Failure to love your neighbor and love God would be an indication that saving faith is not present. People who show no evidence of loving God by serving others may be shocked to find out that Jesus does not know them as His sheep.

But before we go any further we have to look at this from the perspective of the goats and why they were so caught off guard. They would not easily accept the idea that they just talked a good game. In fact, in Matthew 7 they protest rather vigorously any notion that they were nothing but talk. Look at the resumé they put forward: "Lord, didn't we do great works in your name? We preached about you, declared you to be Lord, for crying out loud we even cast out demons in your name." These people were certain they did everything Jesus asked of them and were certain that He had blessed their efforts and their ministry.

It is that aspect of this whole story that makes it so frightening. By all appearances these were successful people in the ministry of God. How could they not be? They went toe to toe with demons and defeated them in Jesus' name. And, notice, Jesus doesn't dispute that claim. He doesn't accuse them of lying or being mistaken. Instead, He simply dismisses that piece of information as irrelevant. It has no bearing on their relationship with Him and their eternal destiny! How can giving demons a beat-down in Jesus' name not be relevant? Certainly if a ministry today was showing that demons were being defeated and a whole host of other incredible things were being done in Jesus' name, people would be convinced that the ministry was blessed by God and the person doing the ministry has had some sort of double anointing of the Holy Spirit.

The problem we have with this text, and the situation it describes, stems from not having a more complete understanding of the Bible. In fact, when we look closer at the ministry of Jesus this situation of "anointed" people doing amazing ministry but not having a relationship of faith with Him is already evident in His lifetime. Consider the life and ministry of Judas and you see what I mean.

Luke 9:1-6 opens up a startling truth. In this passage Jesus sends out the twelve apostles to do ministry. It is all part of the discipleship process Jesus has called them, and us, to participate in. He has been healing people, casting out demons, performing miracles. They have been watching Him do this and from time to time even assisted in the work. Now it is time for them to go and do it. Verse 1 says, *"And he called the twelve together and gave them power and authority over all demons and to cure diseases."* Then verse 6 tells us *"they departed and went through the villages, preaching the gospel and healing everywhere."*

Judas was one of the twelve. He was given the authority to go, preach the gospel in Jesus' name as well as cast out demons and heal people. And you can be certain that it happened. Judas healed people, preached the gospel, and cast out demons in Jesus' name. Nowhere is there any indication that Judas was denied this power or that the other eleven were successful but he was not. Given his later betrayal of Jesus, you can be sure that the writers of Matthew, Mark, Luke, and John would have been more than willing to point out any shortcomings in Judas. They certainly did not hesitate to point out that there was an issue with the group treasury because Judas was pilfering funds. If he tried to heal someone or cast out a demon and it never worked, you can bet it would have been added to the list of his deficiencies. Obviously that never happened.

So here you have Judas, one of the twelve, a man who preached in Jesus' name, cast out demons in Jesus' name, healed people in Jesus' name, yet the Bible says that it would have been better for him if he had never been born. His fate for the betrayal of Christ is such that we should not be surprised to hear Jesus say to Judas, "I never knew you." Yes, Judas did all those things in ministry but clearly he did not "know" Jesus. He was acquainted with Him, familiar with Him, but Judas didn't know Jesus, the Messiah, God come in the flesh, Savior, King, Friend. There was no relational knowledge that stemmed from a heart that loved Jesus.

Here is the bottom-line question on this for me and for you. If a man who spent three years breathing the same air as Jesus, witnessed the raising of Lazarus from the dead, was used to help collect a dozen baskets of leftover food from feeding five thousand people, who cast out demons and healed people by the power of Jesus' name, if that man could be said to not "know" Jesus or be known by Him, what about me? What about you?

The issue is clearly not what you have accomplished in your efforts. You may have built the biggest ministry in the history of the church, preached to millions, written a library full of books on God and the Bible. But it all means nothing if you do not know and are known by Jesus. That means you are in a relationship with Him that is characterized by love. When you look at the things Jesus praised the sheep for, it was all acts of love to people who were not typical recipients of love.

Paul's first letter to the Corinthians contains one of the most-often-read passages in all the Bible. 1 Corinthians 13 is also known as "the love chapter." In it Paul gives a timeless definition of love and its importance. In the first several verses Paul makes it clear that it really doesn't matter what you do in God's name. If you are without love, then you gain nothing.

"If I speak in the tongues of men and of angels, but have not love, I am a noisy gong or a clanging cymbal. And if I have prophetic powers, and understand all mysteries and all knowledge, and if I have all faith, so as to remove mountains, but have not love, I am nothing. If I give away all I have, and if I deliver up my body to be burned, but have not love, I gain nothing" (1 Corinthians 13:1-3).

Look at the list of accomplishments Paul mentions: prophetic powers, all faith, knowledge and understanding, miraculous moving of mountains, and even suffering martyrdom by being burned at the stake. None of those things amount to a hill of beans if you do not have love.

The question needs to be asked, Who or what is to be the object of our love? Love cannot be some nebulous, ethereal feeling with no direction or aim, no recipient of our love. Jesus makes that as clear as possible when He said that the greatest commandment is to love God with all your heart, mind, soul, and strength, and love your neighbor as yourself. All of the commands of God can be fulfilled if we truly love Him and one another. Jesus said that all the law and prophets hang on loving God and loving your neighbor. Think of it like this. You can do all kinds of good deeds but if you do them not out of love but out of your desire to be noticed, or out of guilt, or out of a desire to earn a place in heaven, then you will gain nothing. But, if you strive to love God with all you are, and your neighbor as yourself, you will end up doing all sorts of wonderful acts of love and service, without even thinking about yourself and, ironically, receive a great reward from Jesus. The sheep apparently did that. They had no idea they did all the wonderful things for Jesus that He said they did. They were actually very surprised by His reaction to them. Their love of others was done out of love for them and for Jesus.

The reason Jesus did not accept the goats, or know the people who cried, "Lord, Lord," was because they did not love Him or one another as the Great Commandment calls for. If they did love Him, then He would have known them. Love requires a relationship in which you know the other party. A relationship with Jesus is built on His loving you and you responding in love for Him. Faith is wrapped up in that relationship.

People have the mistaken idea that being a Christian is all about the stuff you do or do not do, all the rules you keep or don't keep. How often you go to church, how many Bible verses you have memorized, whether you drink alcohol or not, which candidate you voted for, and on and on. Jesus said that what identifies us as His followers is far more simple than that. In John 13:35 Jesus says that all men will know that we are His disciples by the love we have for one another. So if the story of the sheep and goats freaks you out and has you wondering, "Have I done enough for Jesus to be sure I am going to heaven?" you need to change the question. Instead, ask yourself, *Do I love Jesus and other people?* That is the real issue. If you love God and your neighbor, there will come a day when Jesus looks you in the eye and says, "I know you!"

CHAPTER 10

FELLOWSHIP WITH GOD REQUIRES SUFFERING

"For it has been granted to you that for the sake of Christ you should not only believe in Him but also suffer for His sake." — Philippians 1:29

"... that I may know him and the power of his resurrection, and may share his sufferings, becoming like him in his death." — Philippians 3:10

"Not only that, but we rejoice in our sufferings, knowing that suffering produces endurance, and endurance produces character, and character produces hope, and hope does not put us to shame, because God's love has been poured into our hearts through the Holy Spirit who has been given to us."
— Romans 5:3-5

WE MET THE FIRST week of sixth grade. I was the new kid in the class, and as it turned out we lived two streets apart. In one of those oddities of life a group of six of us in the neighborhood became friends and all of us had a first name that began with the letter D. So very quickly we all became known by our last name with a D in front. I became D'Lacich and he became D'Johnson. His real name is Dwight and he is my longest-lasting friend, and as such a most treasured friend.

When we were growing up it was all about sports and girls. I won't say anything about the girl part of things, but sports is another matter. We spent lots of time together on the baseball field, the basketball court, the golf course, and the football field. In every instance except football Dwight far surpassed me in ability. The sheer brute force aspect of football served me better than the precision of the other sports. I never could beat him on the golf course, for instance. But I noticed that my game always got better when I played with him. In fact, the best round of golf I ever played was the day before Dwight and Debbie were married. I played out of my mind that day, and still he led the way with a better score.

Many memorable events in our lives were shared events. We woke up in my parents' living room one New Year's Day to the news that our hero, Roberto Clemente, had died in a plane crash while on a mercy mission to Puerto Rico. Dwight was in the room along with two other friends the night I gave my life to Christ. We were in each other's weddings. Like the deepest of friendships, no matter how long the time is between phone calls or dinners, the bond of friendship is still unbreakable.

A few years ago I received the proverbial punch in the gut when I learned that Dwight had just been diagnosed with amyotrophic lateral sclerosis (ALS), otherwise known as Lou Gehrig's disease. There is no cure. The best they can do is manage the pain and the deterioration of the body. The first sign for Dwight that something was wrong was the difficulty he had holding a golf club. In just a year he went from that seemingly minor issue to being in a wheelchair most of the time and needing a neck brace to hold his head up when he worked on his computer.

Six months after the diagnosis, we were together at a charity golf tournament for him and his family. The goal was to raise money for the remodeling of their house to accommodate the inevitable wheelchair. Later we got together again, this time at Super Bowl XLIII in Tampa, Florida. For two die-hard Steelers fans it was a dream come true, especially since they won their sixth Lombardi Trophy. For me, getting a picture with Dwight at that game was more precious than I can describe. The Steelers' victory was an ecstatic experience. Being with Dwight was deeper, more important by far, and will remain etched in my mind like few other events. It is another of those highly valued, shared events.

Whenever someone close to you has a tragedy strike, it must be a nearly universal response to at some point wonder how you would handle that in your own life. I have thought long and hard about how I might handle such an illness for my wife or myself. The way Dwight and Debbie handled the illness that, barring a miracle, would one day end his life has forced me to ask that question over and over again. You see, my friend Dwight loves Jesus with all his heart. It was out of love for Jesus that he and Debbie adopted two little boys with special needs, adding them to their very healthy biological daughter and son. It is out of love for Jesus that he has served in his local church. It is out of love for Jesus that he approached his suffering thinking only about others. I am forced to ask how I would handle such suffering because I see Dwight doing so with dignity and grace, and for the glory of God. In that suffering he challenges me, humbles me, and inspires me to want to honor God, if only in just a fraction of the way he does.

Oftentimes in the face of suffering we play the victim. "Why me?" we ask. "What did I do to deserve this?" We argue with the fairness of it all. In other cases we lapse into depression and give up. Dwight has been all about Jesus getting the glory. His attitude has been that of the Apostle Paul: "Whether I live or die, let God be glorified." Also like Paul, I think Dwight has an even deeper connection to Jesus because of the fellowship shared by those who suffer. Dwight wants Jesus to use his personal experience of suffering to point others to Jesus. I think his love for Jesus is actually growing as a result of that shared fellowship. Dwight understands that God never promised us a life free of suffering, at least not this side of eternity. What He did promise us was that He would be with us always, no matter what. We would be in fellowship with Him always, because He is always with us.

There is a sense in which suffering is the calling of the Christian. Following Jesus does not come with a promise that your problems will disappear and the road of life will be smooth and free from potholes and hazards. It is quite the opposite. Jesus actually promises that if we follow Him people will persecute us. There will be hardship and toil along the way. His rationale is that if the world crucified Him and He is the Lord, how much more will we, the followers, face hardship and strife? The "health and wealth" gospel crowd that tries to show that God only wants you to be free of suffering and blessed by a huge bank account is totally out of touch with the true heart of God, the teaching of the Bible, and the example of great saints from the past.

FINDING JOY IN THE SUFFERING

Paul's letter to the Philippians is a study in how to jam-pack a small letter with huge lessons on the nature of God and following Jesus no matter what. Time and again Paul urges the Philippians to rejoice, and he tells them of his own joy. This comes from a man who is in prison for his faith in Jesus and facing the very real possibility of being beheaded any day. In just four short chapters Paul talks in depth about joy and suffering. He actually embraces the suffering not as something to be endured but as something to be welcomed as a badge of honor.

Paul said that we are to embrace our suffering as something that has been granted to us in Christ (Philippians 1:29). If someone gives you a grant, they are giving you something desirable. If your request is granted, then you have received something good. If you submit a grant proposal for funding and get it, you have been given a good thing. Paul says that our suffering in Christ is something with which we have been "granted." He connects the blessing of the "suffering grant" with the blessings of believing in Jesus. In fact, he seems to think of suffering in Christ as an added bonus that goes above and beyond the basics of a relationship of faith in Christ: It has been granted to you not *only* to believe in Jesus but *also* to have fellowship with Him in His suffering.

There is something about suffering for our faith, or as part of life in general, that unites us to Jesus in an even tighter bond than simply believing in Him. It is true of our relationship with Jesus and it is evident in our relationships with one another. Soldiers who have suffered together through the horrors of war have a bond with one another that others can never have. Cancer survivors have a bond with other cancer survivors that is deeper and tighter than everyday human relationships. Parents who have lost a child through death have a bond with similar parents that goes far beyond the normal bonds of joy that all parents share.

In these and other examples of suffering, people who have no other possible connection with each other—in fact, people who would by most human standards not want anything to do with each other—become the deepest of friends. The white soldier from segregated 1960s' Alabama becomes a lifelong friend with the black soldier from Detroit, each willing to die for the other. The cancer survivor volunteers countless hours to counsel and befriend those who have just been given their own devastating news. The parent whose child died five years ago sacrificially serves the family fresh in its grief, in spite of the fact that they never met before.

Suffering has its own fellowship. Jesus came as what Isaiah 53 refers to as The Suffering Servant. He came to give His life as a ransom for many. We can experience a certain level of connection with Jesus when we trust Him by faith. That relationship deepens when we fellowship with Him in our suffering.

In the early days of the church, following the resurrection and ascension of Jesus, the apostles faced serious persecution for their faith in Jesus. Luke tells us in Acts 5:17-42 that they were arrested for preaching about Jesus and told to stop. Before being released they were severely beaten for their faith. If this happened to Christians in America today, we would be on the phone to a lawyer so fast it would make your head spin. Our anger and indignation would be astronomical. But that was not the reaction of the apostles. Acts 5:41-42 records: *"Then they left the presence of the council, rejoicing that they were counted worthy to suffer dishonor for the name [of Jesus]. And every day in the temple and from house to house, they did not cease teaching and preaching Jesus as the Christ."*

They rejoiced because they were counted worthy to suffer dishonor for the name of Jesus. Suffering for the name of Jesus did not cause them to question their relationship with God. They didn't cry out to God asking why they had been abandoned to suffering. That is how we react. Instead they praised God because their suffering for the cause of Christ was a stamp of approval, it was a powerful affirmation that they were, in fact, connected to Christ. How different is that from us today. We suffer and we complain that God has abandoned us. They suffered and they praised God, rejoicing for having the privilege of being so closely connected to Christ that they could suffer dishonor for Him.

SUFFERING FOR THE GLORY OF GOD

In the prosperity gospel movement there is a way of looking at the Christian life that sees health, prosperity, and a victorious life as the way God will be glorified and people will come to Jesus. The idea is simple. If people see how great and blessed the Christian life can be, then they will want to follow Jesus. In this way of thinking, God is most glorified when we are most blessed with health and wealth. If you are sick or poor, or both, then this is seen as being a disgraceful thing. Something must be wrong if you are not healthy and wealthy. There is nothing wrong with God, but rather something is wrong with you. You must have some deep sin in your life that is preventing God from healing you or blessing you.

In John 9, Jesus is confronted with a dilemma. There is a grown man who was born blind. People are perplexed about why he was born this way. They have the same mindset as the prosperity gospel folks. Some person's sin is responsible for this blindness. The problem is figuring out whose sin is to blame. They have a hard time blaming it on the man born blind. After all, how much sin could he have committed in the womb? So, clearly the sin was not the blind man's. So then it must be his parents' fault. But what kind of God would cause a person to live in blindness because their parents committed some sin before they were ever born? It was a real theological conundrum.

Jesus, as He so often does, proposes a different way. *"Jesus answered, 'It was not that this man sinned or his parents, but that the works of God might be displayed in him'"* (John 9:3). Do you catch the stunning thing that Jesus is saying? This man, who has suffered with blindness from birth, who has never seen the smile of his parents, who has heard the mocking of people convinced he was being punished for sin, who has been forced to beg for scraps to feed himself, who has been bruised and battered throughout his life, stumbling into and over chairs and rocks and stumps, this man who has suffered so much has suffered it so that on this day the works of God might be displayed in him. Are you kidding me? God caused this man to suffer so much so that when he finally met Jesus, after years of blindness, he would be healed and God glorified?

God uses the suffering of His people to bring glory to Himself. In other words, God uses the suffering of His people so that others will be led to worship and praise Him. Sometimes God does it through healing just like with the man born blind. The people were amazed, stunned, shocked, saying they had never seen anything like this before. But sometimes God brings glory to Himself by the way He uses suffering to shape us more and more into the kind of people whose very lives will glorify God.

When people look at my friend Dwight and his wife they can't help but notice that they are approaching his illness, including all the hardship and adjustments it requires, as a way to point people to Jesus. Dwight is determined to show people that a follower of Jesus approaches suffering and death in a far different way than someone who does not know Jesus. They approach life and death with a joy that makes no sense, unless you account for the power of the Holy Spirit to strengthen and uphold you. Their joy points people directly to the reality of God and the presence of Jesus in their lives. Dwight and Debbie have found their greatest joy and pleasure in life within their relationship with Christ. The suffering they have gone through has actually made that joy deeper than ever. Jesus is more real to them in the midst of suffering than He ever was in the midst of blessing. God has been glorified in the fellowship of their suffering and they have grown in Christ more than ever before.

This shouldn't surprise us. In Romans 5, Paul gives us a series of growth steps that have their foundation in our suffering: *"We rejoice in our sufferings, knowing that suffering produces endurance, and endurance produces character, and character produces hope, and hope does not put us to shame"* (Romans 5:3-5).

The struggles that we face in life serve to make us stronger in our faith and more like Christ, if we allow them. Each struggle prepares us for the next level of becoming like Jesus. In trying to bypass, avoid, or ignore the lessons of suffering we risk greater dangers later in life. When I was in grade school we had a science experiment in the back of the classroom. It was a group of chicken eggs in an incubator. Each day we checked the incubator to see if there was any sign of a baby chick starting to break through the shell. Finally, one day during class, the person sitting nearest the incubator heard a small tapping, cracking noise. Suddenly the whole class jumped up from our seats to watch the long-awaited event. As the baby chick struggled to free itself from the shell it was clear that it was an agonizing and difficult task. One of the students asked if we shouldn't help by taking off some of the shell. The teacher told us that if we did this it would make it easier for the chick to get out but in the long run it would be very damaging. The chick needed to struggle through the suffering time in order to strengthen the muscles it needed to survive. The struggle of getting out of the shell was actually designed to prepare the chick for the life ahead. God has designed our suffering in just the same way.

The apostles considered it a privilege to suffer for Jesus. In that suffering there was a renewed sense of being united with Him and of pointing people towards Him. Dwight Johnson is doing that every day. The more his body deteriorates, the more glory he brings to Jesus by living a life that loves Jesus above all else.

The more I think about Dwight the more I am forced to smile. He was better than me at baseball, basketball, and golf. Now it appears he is better than me at being a Christian as well. He is bringing glory to God in a situation that I don't know how I would handle. However, I do know this: when the time comes when I must face that kind of suffering, I know that my game will be better because of Dwight. Some things never change.

UPDATE:

Tuesday, February 1, 2011: I visited Dwight for the last time, in this life anyway. There have been so many people coming to see Dwight that Deb arranged for me and Dwight to have a few hours alone. The reason this was the last visit is the breathing apparatus that he has been using is no longer helping. The next option is a tracheotomy, to put him on a ventilator. Dwight and Deb decided long ago that when it reached this point they would not take that option. There is no point. Dwight is ready to go. They are going to remove the breathing assist. Dwight is so ready he decided not to wait to see the Steelers play the Packers in the Super Bowl on Sunday. They will remove the breathing apparatus on Thursday. I told him I understand: for all the glory that is the Steelers and Super Bowls, the glory of heaven outshines that in ways indescribable.

I have to admit that my emotions bounce from moment to moment. One moment it's joy at the picture of Dwight with Jesus. The next is emptiness at the sense of a page turning in my own life and the resulting void, then to anger and frustration and wanting to break something, and then back to joy. But this is not about me. I find myself regularly having to remind myself of that. It is about Dwight and Deb and the incredible way in which they have dealt with this as they love and worship Jesus. As I say goodbye Dwight looks me in the eye and says, "I love you." I lean down, tell him that I love him, and kiss the top of his balding head. I turn and walk down the long hallway and make a very long and lonely drive from Gainesville back home to Orlando. It's only two hours but I found myself meandering through backcountry roads and taking four hours instead. Driving down I-75 in the midst of heavy traffic, speeding trucks, and anxious tourists just didn't appeal to me.

Thursday, February 3, 2011: This morning the medical team took Dwight off the breathing mask, gave him some medication to keep him comfortable, and waited until the CO_2 levels rose to the point that he slept and slipped away into the arms of Jesus. It took a few hours. But those hours were filled with songs of worship to God, lots of prayer, and tears of pain and joy.

I am regularly reminded of the power of suffering in Christ when I think of what Deb said to me at the end of my last visit with Dwight: *"I know that God is real if for no other reason than the unexplainable peace that washes over me when I picture Dwight with Jesus."*

Amen to that.

CHAPTER 11

JESUS CAME TO DIVIDE PEOPLE

" 'Do not think that I have come to bring peace to the earth. I have not come to bring peace, but a sword. For I have come to set a man against his father, and a daughter against her mother, and a daughter-in-law against her mother-in-law.' " — Matthew 10:34-35

"The messengers of Jesus will be hated to the end of time. They will be blamed for all the division which rends cities and homes. Jesus and his disciples will be condemned on all sides for undermining family life, and for leading the nation astray; they will be called crazy fanatics and disturbers of the peace." — Dietrich Bonhoeffer

THERE IS A CLEAR IMPRESSION of Jesus as being very mild-mannered, kind and caring, a person who reconciles people to one another and to God. There is a certain sense in which that is true. He certainly came to reconcile us to God and one another. Yet in another sense the mission of Jesus is one of division. He says that He came to set men at variance with one another. In some way, because of Jesus, even close family members will be at odds with one another.

When I gave my life to Christ things began to change very quickly. Some friends who I used to get drunk with in high school had a hard time accepting the changes, and honestly I didn't always do the best job of communicating or living this newfound faith in the early days. My relationship with Christ also had a huge impact on my family relationships. The heart of the conflict was that by following Jesus I had adopted a new Lord and Master. My view of the world began to change. My values changed. My priorities changed. My ambitions changed. There was a growing gap that developed between me and my dad in particular. His hopes for my life—to be in business and make lots of money—were no longer my hopes, if they ever were. When I had been a Christian for less than eighteen months I sensed God calling me to a life of serving Him. I was in my first semester at college, sitting at my desk studying for a mid-term exam, and knew with every fiber in my being that God spoke to me and said, "Study for me." I can still picture the textbook I was reading, the position of the desk in the room, and even the lamp on the desk. I knew in that moment that a fundamental shift had just taken place.

There were two issues that had to be dealt with in that call from God. The first was that I knew I could not stay at the school I was attending and continue as a special education major. I needed to get somewhere that I could get an education in the things of God. Not having a church background or any direction made that an uncertain journey.

The second issue was the need to let my dad know of the change in my plans. After some serious conversations, with it being obvious that I was committed to this new journey, my dad made one request: that in addition to my pursuit of a degree in theology that I also get something practical to go with it. To him, theology was all theory and there was no chance of actually making a living. So I transferred schools and was a double major in theology and psychology. I suppose he had thoughts that at least I might become a psychologist someday and that would be a decent living. Even though he agreed to the plan, it was clear that he was not happy with it. Years later he opened up about that and told me that when I came home from college with my plan to go into ministry, I could not have hurt him more if I had kicked him in the groin. Clearly my path of following Jesus had put me at variance with my dad.

Over the years that variance would surface occasionally. He would have some plan for me to get rich, which usually involved some type of pyramid scheme with people in the congregations I served. That was obviously not an option. When my wife, Barb, and I had our first son, and then eighteen months later had number two, my dad was convinced that I was being as irresponsible and wrong-headed as anyone could be. I was making $14,000 a year and here we were bringing kids into the world. Our values and worldviews were miles apart.

There was probably no more telling incident of that separation than the period of time when the boys were little and I wasn't even sure where my dad lived. We saw him occasionally. He would stop by to see Barb and me, as well as Zack and Justin, and newborn son number three, Garrett. But he was always very coy about where he was living. That went on for several months, until one day, in circumstances that I can't even remember, I found out where he lived. It was an apartment building that I could see from my kitchen window. We were only two hundred yards from one another, yet clearly we were light years apart.

If we are going to follow Jesus and have Him truly be our Lord, then there will be times when people who do not follow Him will not understand us. There will be times when they will be angry with us, hurt by us, argue with us. We must realize that when we follow Jesus we become citizens of His kingdom. We become exiles in our own communities. We just don't exactly fit anymore. That misfit will divide us from others. But it need not make us people who lash out against those who are different from us. Paul tells us in Romans 12:18: "If possible, so far as it depends on you, be at peace with all men." By its very nature, our following of Jesus puts us at odds. But in spite of that reality, we are to do all that we possibly can to bridge the gap and be reconciled in Christ.

Sadly, there are many people who are trying to follow Christ and they end up at odds with people and divided from those not following Christ not because the cross is an offense, or a biblical worldview necessarily separates them, but because they seem to be doing everything they can to not live at peace with all men. It is one thing to humbly and lovingly follow Jesus, have to stand your ground on something, and have it bring division in your family or with friends. Jesus is saying that is simply part of the deal when we follow Him. It happens. But it is another thing entirely if the reason for the division between you and other people is not because of the gospel but because you are being a jerk. Constantly berating people who are not following Jesus, or who are not following Him the way you think they should, is sure to put a division between you. Our call from Jesus is not to condemn and berate, but to lovingly reach out to people and let the cross of Christ and the scandal of it be the only thing that causes division.

In the case of my dad it took years of Barb and me faithfully living out our relationship with Christ, being patient and as loving as we could, before anything changed in my dad. It meant that at times we put ourselves at odds with him. Our worldviews were just so different that he could not understand why we lived as we did. In fact, he was certain that we were being irresponsible by not trying to get as rich as possible as quickly as possible. But over time he began to see something. He saw that our children were happy even though they did not have all the stuff he thought they should. He saw that our family was content even though our cars were old and our house was the poster child of the handyman special. He saw that Barb and I deeply loved one another in a way that he felt he was missing in his relationships. Things began to change. He started asking questions about the ministry and the church

I served. First the questions were more in the area of things he could understand: How did we plan our budget? What was the process we went through to hire an architect and builder when we built a new worship center? But eventually it turned to questions of belief and a relationship with God. The division that existed because Barb and I put Jesus first was slowly being overcome by prayer and patient faithfulness.

The real turning point came shortly after my dad had heart surgery. He had suffered a major heart attack and was within seconds of the doctors giving up on him when his heart started back up. The surgery became needed if he was going to avoid another heart attack. Following the surgery he had a few weeks in which he felt better than he had in years. That all changed when he got a call from his doctor. Some of the follow-up blood work revealed that he contracted acute leukemia. There was very little hope; even though he went through all the chemo and every possible treatment, within nine months he died.

That diagnosis, and the months that followed, became the tool God used to completely remove the division. My dad came to the realization that he needed the Jesus I knew. I received a call that I needed to get to my dad's house right away, because the end was near. When I arrived I was stunned to find him sitting up at the foot of his bed. I squatted down in front of him with my back to the wall as he spoke to me:

"What do you think, buddy?"

"I think you're coming to the end, Dad."

"You need to tell me what to do."

"We've talked about that before, Dad. You need to give your heart to Jesus."

"OK. Can I have a ham sandwich?"

Yes, my father is on the point of death, asking about his eternal destiny, and in the middle of it all wants a ham sandwich. I looked at his wife, who had this questioning expression on her face, and simply said, "It can't hurt him." So my dad had a few bites of a ham sandwich and then laid down on the bed.

At this point he reached out his hand to me in a sign that I knew meant he wanted to pray. I took his hand, praying desperately in my heart for the right words to share so my dad would finally give his life to Christ. Before I ever had a chance to say anything I heard him say these words, "Jesus I am trusting in you. I put my life in your hands and I want to go to be with you." In that moment the sword of division between my dad and me was removed. He was reconciled to Jesus and that reconciliation meant that nothing stood between us any longer.

It was the last time we spoke. A few moments later he said he wanted to sleep. During the night my dad went to be with Jesus.

By the very nature of who Jesus is, and your commitment to Him above all others, people will be at odds with you. Dietrich Bonhoeffer understood this. He knew that the opposition people have to Jesus would naturally fall on His followers. As we align ourselves with Jesus it means we will stand opposite those who oppose Him. Our relationship with Jesus will cause divisions in our relationships. Jesus knew this as well and expected it. He demanded that, like the first of the Ten Commandments, we would "have no other gods before Him." He demands primacy of relationship, and that conflicts with what others may want from us. Division is inevitable.

It is hard for people to accept that following a loving God can result in division and separation. Certainly there is far more division than can be justified from Scripture, because we at times act in ungodly ways. But there will be times when your devotion to God will and must result in you being at odds with people you love deeply. But never forget that we follow a God of redemption and reconciliation. By the very nature of His death on the cross, His resurrection, and ascension, Jesus makes it possible for people to be reconciled to one another and to Himself. That reconciliation brings us closer to one another than we ever could be without Him. Our role in that reconciliation process is to live out the gospel with as much passion and devotion as possible, to be totally devoted to Jesus—not compromising the truth, yet always speaking it in love. God can use that kind of devotion to Him first in order to show others the way back to Him.

Chapter 12

EVERYTHING RISES AND FALLS ON THE RESURRECTION

"And if Christ has not been raised, then our preaching is in vain and your faith is in vain. We are even found to be misrepresenting God, because we testified about God that he raised Christ, whom he did not raise if it is true that the dead are not raised. For if the dead are not raised, not even Christ has been raised. And if Christ has not been raised, your faith is futile and you are still in your sins. Then those also who have fallen asleep in Christ have perished. If in Christ we have hope in this life only, we are of all people most to be pitied." — 1 Corinthians 15:14-19

"And entering the tomb, they saw a young man sitting on the right side, dressed in a white robe, and they were alarmed. And he said to them, 'Do not be alarmed. You seek Jesus of Nazareth, who was crucified. He has risen; he is not here. See the place where they laid him.' "— Mark 16:5-7

"Suggesting a married Jesus is one thing, but questioning the Resurrection undermines the very heart of Christian belief." — Dan Brown (author of *The Da Vinci Code*)

WHILE WORKING ON MY master's degree, I had a conversation with another student about the resurrection of Jesus. She made a statement that at first might seem to indicate an incredibly strong faith in God: "If the body of Jesus was found in a tomb somewhere, it would not shake my faith at all." Far from this being an example of incredible faith, however, I found it to be the height of both hubris and folly. Hubris because it dared to claim a greater faith than even the Apostle Paul could admit for himself. Folly because that same Paul said that if Jesus is in fact not risen from the dead, then we are to be pitied above all men.

Paul put it this way when he wrote to the Christians in the Greek city of Corinth:

> *"And if Christ has not been raised, then our preaching is in vain and your faith is in vain. We are even found to be misrepresenting God, because we testified about God that he raised Christ, whom he did not raise if it is true that the dead are not raised. For if the dead are not raised, not even Christ has been raised. And if Christ has not been raised, your faith is futile and you are still in your sins. Then those also who have fallen asleep in Christ have perished"* (1 Corinthians 15:14-18).

The fellow student who said that her faith would not be shaken if Jesus had never risen did not understand the absolutely crucial, linchpin place that the resurrection has for followers of Jesus. Paul understood that the resurrection was the game-changer. Because Jesus rose from the dead, everything was now different. It was the resurrection that vindicated Jesus after His humiliating death on the cross. It was the resurrection that demonstrated His victory over sin and death. It was the resurrection that led to His being seated at the right hand of the Father, and at whose name every knee would bow and every tongue confess that Jesus Christ is Lord.

If the resurrection had never happened, then Jesus was simply one more religious teacher who led people astray, only to disappoint them in the end. Rabbi Gamaliel understood this when, in Acts 5, he told the religious leaders to leave the disciples alone. He said that if Jesus was a nobody who was still in the grave, then this talk of Him as a messiah would fade away, just like it had so many times before with other religious zealots. Paul understood that if the resurrection had never really happened then the whole Christian faith was a sham. It was people preaching lies about God. It meant that their faith was only a faith for this life, and that was a huge waste of time and effort.

But Paul was adamant that the resurrection was real; Jesus had risen from the dead. His resurrection was the down payment for us, the guarantee that all who have faith in Jesus will also rise from the dead one day. Jesus is the pioneer who leads the way for all who trust in Him and in the reality of His resurrection.

My friend from graduate school is someone who Paul would say is to be most pitied. She has a faith that really has no future. It is a faith that does not need a risen savior. But without a risen savior, one who is still in the grave, there is only the grave for us. Our faith is for this life only. If Jesus had never been risen, then there is no reason to follow Him. He is just a guy who died two thousand years ago and is still dead. And no matter how much we believe in Him, when we die we will be just as dead for just as long—and stay that way. No hope. No future. No life eternal. If Jesus is still in the grave, then Christianity is a giant lie.

But because He is risen we have life and hope, and a future that is beyond our most vivid and beautiful imaginations. We have a purpose in this life that will find its fulfillment in the next. We have a God who is worthy of our adoration and praise. We have a message to take to people that can change their lives, now and forever. We have a relationship with a very real God who loves us enough to pay the ultimate price for our reconciliation with Him. We have the power to bring that reconciliation to the world, healing to the broken, dignity to the oppressed, joy to the grieving, and laughter to those who weep. I could go on and on, because the resurrection changes everything. From the moment He burst forth from the tomb nothing would ever be the same again. A world that was spiraling down into darkness and oblivion became a world that could be lifted higher and more glorious, all because He is risen.

THE SHOCKING NATURE OF THE RESURRECTION

In order to understand why the resurrection of Jesus is the linchpin to the entire Christian faith we have to put ourselves in the sandals of that small band of disciples who spent so much time with Him in life and then saw Him crucified and buried. Unfortunately for many people raised in a Christian environment or even a culture heavily influenced by Christianity, the resurrection of Jesus has become something of a cliché or simply another miracle like so many He performed.

In some ways, I think the trouble actually begins in childhood. When you are a child everything is possible. Of course your toys talk and play with one another when you leave the room. Obviously animals talk to one another and to humans. Clearly a mermaid can become a person. Of course Jesus can rise from the dead. On one hand such childlike faith is honorable and commendable. Jesus seemed to think so. But the downside is that as we grow and should become more amazed at the provocative nature of the resurrection, we instead are so familiar with it that it never gains the prominence it should have.

I was reminded of this with a recent viewing of a new television series called *Resurrection*. The premise of the show is that a small town undergoes a shocking experience when people who have been long dead and buried start showing up alive, at the same age they were when they died. Part of the plot line is how relatives and loved ones struggle when suddenly confronted with the now-living person, totally healthy and normal. It is a shock to the system that is hard to imagine. People in the town are understandably freaked out by it. Parents will not let their children play with children who have come back from the dead. They can't handle it. Some of the people who have had a loved one return go from shock and disbelief to amazing wonder and joy. They will never be the same.

That was the way it was for the first group of Christ-followers. They knew Jesus was dead. Some of them watched Him die. They heard the last few words forced out of His aching lungs. They saw the light fade from His eyes as He gave up His spirit. They saw the blood flow from His side when the Roman soldier thrust a spear between His ribs and into His heart. They watched as His lifeless body was removed from the cross and placed in a fresh-cut tomb. They shuddered as the heavy stone was rolled into place and set with a loud thud, a finality that could not be undone.

What they experienced was what so many have experienced. You may have been bedside when someone you love was struggling to breathe their last breath. You listened intently as they whispered their final words. You heard the death rattle of their final gasp, and watched as the light faded from their eyes. You stood over their open casket, praying, remembering, grieving. You watched as the casket was closed. The gentle click of the lock startled you with its sharpness, echoing through the room. You stood next to the open grave as they lowered the casket into a finality all its own that could not be undone.

Now imagine that three days later there is a knock at the door and that loved one is standing before you, living, breathing, talking, and asking to come in and have breakfast. After they revive you and pick you up off the floor, and you come to the conclusion that this is real and they are indeed alive, you will never, ever be the same again. Everything will have changed. All your preconceived notions about life, death, and the world will have changed. You will reorient your entire life and worldview around the fact of this resurrection. Your joy and courage will be off the charts. You will be sold out to the risen one, no matter what.

That and more is what happened with the first followers of Jesus. They lived every day in the power of the resurrection of Jesus. A day would not go by when they were not reminded of the fact that Jesus was alive and they had been forgiven. When they sat and broke bread together it was in the joyful knowledge that they broke bread with Him on the night before His death and on the days following His resurrection. The resurrection convinced them that He was more than the Messiah they hoped for. He was God come in the flesh. The resurrection convinced Thomas to fall at the feet of Jesus and declare, "My Lord and my God."

KEEP THE MAIN THING THE MAIN THING

I have countless conversations with people about the Bible, faith, religion, and the existence of God. It is very easy for people to get lost in the weeds of details and philosophical arguments over the Bible, God, suffering, evolution, and a host of other things. What I always try to do is get back to the main issue. Jesus is unique in all of history as one who claimed to be God and backed it up by rising from the dead. Buddha didn't. Mohammed didn't. Moses didn't. Other than Jesus, no one did. That is the crux of it all. If Jesus is risen, then everything changes.

SECTION TWO: YOUR RELATIONSHIP WITH OTHERS

CHAPTER 13

LOVE YOUR ENEMIES

" 'You have heard that it was said, "You shall love your neighbor and hate your enemy." But I say to you, Love your enemies and pray for those who persecute you, so that you may be sons of your Father who is in heaven. For he makes his sun rise on the evil and on the good, and sends rain on the just and on the unjust.' " — Matthew 5:43-45

"But God shows his love for us in that while we were still sinners, Christ died for us. Since, therefore, we have now been justified by his blood, much more shall we be saved by him from the wrath of God. For if while we were enemies we were reconciled to God by the death of his Son, much more, now that we are reconciled, shall we be saved by his life." — Romans 5:8-10

"The Bible tells us to love our neighbors, and also to love our enemies; probably because generally they are the same people." — G.K. Chesterton

THE COMMAND JESUS GIVES us to love our enemies is impossible to obey. It just can't be done. How in the world is it possible to overcome the hurt, fear, anguish, pain, suffering, rage, and bitterness that is foisted upon us because of enemies who hate us? Love my enemies? Are you serious? My first reaction is to want to feast on their bones and drag their women and children off into slavery. Well, maybe that is a bit much, but you get the idea. Everything within us says that there is no way on God's green earth that we are ever going to love our enemies, and God should understand that. Loving your enemies is just impossible. Or is it?

Let's think for a minute about what we mean by love. Maybe, just maybe, the issue is not with the impossibility of loving our enemy. Maybe the issue is that we don't understand what Jesus was asking for when He said we are to love our enemies. Just what do we think love is? If I look at cultural images that seek to clarify and define love, I am convinced that our definition of love is the issue. Think about all the situations in which we use the word love.

"I love mushroom-Swiss hamburgers."

"I love it when the Steelers defense shuts down opposing quarterbacks by pummeling them into the turf."

"I love our 115-pound Rhodesian Ridgeback hound dog."

"I love reading Bernard Cornwell novels."

"I love sitting on the back porch trimming my bonsai trees."

"I love my wife."

"I love Jesus."

The list could go on and on but I think you get the idea. Hopefully I mean something very different when I say, "I love the Steelers' defense," and when I say, "I love my wife." Hopefully my relationship with Jesus is on a different level than my relationship with a hamburger topped with Swiss cheese and cultivated fungus. Looking at such common uses for the word "love" tells me nothing about what we think love is. When you love everything it amounts to meaning that you really love nothing. If you love everything without distinction, then love is meaningless, there is no value to it.

In romantic relationships people talk about "falling" in love. I think this might get us closer to the unspoken, culturally accepted definition of love. People see someone from across the room and boom! Something out of nowhere swoops in and grabs hold of their entire body. They start to feel a little bit warm all over, a little weak in the knees, a bit of fluttering in the stomach. They can't take their eyes off the person. Every image of them brings an uncontrollable smile to their face. Then they begin spending time with the object of this love and it gets even more intense. Their heart beats a little faster with every word they exchange. When they kiss for the first time, somewhere fireworks blaze across the sky and angels burst forth in song. At some point they "make love," which in itself should cause us to ask what those previous feelings really were, if now we are "making" love. If we are making it, did we or did we not have it before?

Still, the feelings of ecstasy and delight continue for some time. The length of time seems inversely proportional to how famous you are, or if you star in your own reality cable TV show. At some point those infamous words are spoken: "It's just not the same anymore. I have fallen out of love with you." Suddenly the thrill is gone. The fireworks have fizzled. The angels are singing off-key. Love, like Elvis, has somehow mysteriously left the building. Love in our modern—and now post-modern—world is nothing more than the emotional boost of pleasure that we get from someone else's company. It is nothing but a feeling of delight that we experience from another.

That kind of love is impossible to give to an enemy. When love is seen as nothing more than a fleeting emotion that we can't control, that we fall in and out of, and that comes and goes in a completely arbitrary way, then it is impossible to obey the command of Jesus to love our enemies. You cannot love someone if love is beyond your ability to manage or manufacture.

Either something is seriously wrong with our understanding of love, or something is seriously wrong with Jesus. I think we all know that answer to that. We don't want to admit it, but our understanding of love is seriously flawed. It is so flawed that I propose we have accepted a cheap, satanic counterfeit for love and have been duped into thinking it is the epitome of love.

Jesus did not command us to feel a certain way about our enemies. Instead, Jesus gives us a command that directs how we are to treat people with whom we have major conflicts, no matter how we feel about them. His command to love our enemies comes in the midst of the Sermon on the Mount. In that message He has already told us that when we are sued for one thing, we should willingly give up even more. He also said that when someone forces us to do go a mile in order to serve them, then we should volunteer to go an extra mile. It is a series of statements about the need to sacrifice our own comfort and position and avoid emotional knee-jerk reactions in order to demonstrate a Christ-like character. The command to love our enemies is one more example in that chain of difficult behavioral commands.

Although love certainly has an emotional facet to it, it is also a verb, an action that we are to carry out. When Paul tells husbands to "love their wives as Christ loved the church by laying down His life for her," he doesn't say to do that only when they have warm, fuzzy feelings. He is saying that we love someone by the way we treat them no matter how we feel about them. One way of understanding what Jesus is saying when He tells us to love our enemies is that we are to "be loving" towards them, by showing them the kindness that we would want shown to us. Jesus is including even our enemies in the definition of who the neighbor is that we are to love. We are to love them as we love ourselves.

He goes on to tell us to pray for those who persecute us. Your first emotional reaction might be to pray that God strikes them down and vindicates you. But when Jesus tells us to pray for those enemies who persecute us, He is telling us to pray that God blesses them. He is telling us to pray that God pours His grace upon them and leads them to a relationship with Him. He is telling us to pray for them in a way that love demands.

In doing this Jesus says we will show that we are children of our heavenly Father. That is what this is all about. How we respond to our enemies should demonstrate who God is. Our own feelings of anger and revenge and hurt are inconsequential compared to the opportunity we have to show people who our Father is and bring Him glory. Our desire to get back at an enemy should be trumped by our desire that God would be honored and glorified, and that more and more people would go from being His enemy to being His follower and friend.

Several years ago I was faced with a person who said and did some things that unjustly caused incredible pain for my family and me. My desire was to strike back, but somehow God's grace kept me from doing so. When his own life started to spin out of control and fall apart I did all I could to show this other person grace and mercy whenever I ran into him in the community. After two years he got in touch with me to ask forgiveness. He was trying to get his life back in order and get right with God. He told me that the grace I showed him was crucial in causing him to admit his own sin and turn back to Jesus. It was the love of Christ that made the difference. I could have reacted out of my emotion of hurt and anger, or I could have acted with the love of Christ. Letting the love of Christ come through saved me from a life of bitterness and him from a life of estrangement from God.

What motivated me time and again in that situation was the realization that such grace was exactly how God treated me when I was His enemy. The Bible makes it clear that prior to coming to faith in Christ, I was God's enemy:

"But God shows his love for us in that while we were still sinners, Christ died for us. Since, therefore, we have now been justified by his blood, much more shall we be saved by him from the wrath of God. For if while we were enemies we were reconciled to God by the death of his Son, much more, now that we are reconciled, shall we be saved by his life" (Romans 5:8-10).

Jesus calls us to love our enemies and has every right to do so, because He did that for us without hesitation. People rarely view themselves as being God's enemy. It is just not something we think about ourselves. At worst, people feel like they don't have much of a relationship or interest in God, but enemies is not in the equation. We think that enemies must be at war with one another, out to do one another in. Certainly that is not how most people approach their relationship with God. Yet, the Bible says that before being reconciled to God through faith in Christ, we are in fact God's enemies. How can that be? It's not like you have been shaking your fist at God in a rage, calling on Him to do battle with you on some cosmic scale.

From the fifties through to the eighties, the United States and the Soviet Union were at war. It wasn't a shooting war, or what people called a hot war. It was one in which we didn't shoot at one another, at least not directly. But the two nations were clearly not at peace. It was the two big boys on the block knowing that one day they were going to have to either start throwing punches or one of them was going to have to back down and concede the rule of the block to the other. We called it The Cold War. There was no direct shooting, but neither was there peace. At least there was no peace in the biblical idea of "shalom." Shalom is not just the absence of hostilities. It is the presence of reconciliation and of a relationship of honor, respect, love, and caring. In God's categories, we are either in a state of shalom or war. It may be a cold war. We may not be lobbing grenades at God, but we are certainly not in a state of shalom with Him. The only way that comes about is because Jesus loved His enemies—us—to the point of going to the cross, in order to reconcile us to God and move us from the category of enemies, to that of people living in shalom with God.

That is what loving your enemies is all about. It is about bringing real peace between you and the people with whom you are at war. Jesus went to the cross not just so you could be reconciled to God, your enemy, but so that you could also be reconciled to the enemy next door, or in the office across the hall, or the family member who hurt you so deeply years ago.

What does it look like to love your enemy? The Bible gives us some very practical examples. The overarching idea comes from Jesus in Luke 6:35: *"But love your enemies, and do good, and lend, expecting nothing in return, and your reward will be great, and you will be sons of the Most High, for he is kind to the ungrateful and the evil."* This verse comes in the context of how to treat people who treat you badly. Jesus is saying that loving them, your enemy, should come under the rubric of doing good things for them. In fact, He says that we should be willing to do provocatively good things for them. For instance, He says be willing to lend them money without expecting to get paid back, ever. Clearly, loving your enemies is not about how you feel towards them, but about what you do for them.

Loving your enemies is not just a New Testament concept. It is given to us from the earliest pages of God's Word. From Moses we get clear examples of what it means to love your enemy in practical ways. Take this example from Exodus 23:4-5:

"If you meet your enemy's ox or his donkey going astray, you shall bring it back to him. If you see the donkey of one who hates you lying down under its burden, you shall refrain from leaving him with it; you shall rescue it with him."

I don't know about you, but my inclination is that if I see my enemy's donkey wandering away, getting lost, I think I would be thrilled and consider it God's justice. If I saw my neighbor's donkey weighed down under its burden, unable to get up and move, and my neighbor struggling mightily to deal with it, I would laugh thinking what an idiot he was for piling so much stuff on the poor creature. In a current day example it would be as if I was driving in a typical Florida summer rainstorm, while my neighbor is at the side of the road with a flat tire, clearly having issues with it, and I drive past laughing that what goes around comes around.

God will have none of that. Just as in Exodus, God's people were called to love their enemies by serving them in their time of need, so God's people today are called to love their enemies by doing the same. That loving service can be helping change a flat tire, providing a meal in time of sickness, cutting the lawn when they are on vacation, or an endless list of other acts of kindness.

THE POWER OF COGNITIVE DISSONANCE

You may ask, What's the point? Why should I bother loving my enemy? After all, they don't care a bit about me and certainly wouldn't stop to help me with a flat tire, in the rain, on a speedy interstate highway. The answer to the why question is two-fold, and both parts have to do with the power of cognitive dissonance and God's ultimate desire for us.

"Cognitive dissonance" is the term that describes what happens in our thinking when two things just do not fit together in our mind. "Cognitive" has to do with thinking and "dissonance" has to do with fit. For instance, a dissonant chord in music is one that just doesn't fit. Think of it as the opposite of harmony.

Psychologists have noticed that we do not like to have ideas in our head that don't fit together. We want things to be in harmony. And we will go through great mental gymnastics in order to bring about cognitive harmony. One of the points related to this is that psychologists have learned that we generally find it easier to change our minds than change our behavior. As a result there are times when, if we are forced to adopt a behavior that conflicts with a cognitive stance in our minds, we will eventually change our minds in order to resolve the conflict or dissonance.

For instance, if you force two prejudicial people into a situation in which they are forced to depend on and watch out for one another—in a military unit, for example—over time you will find those two people becoming less and less prejudicial. Their experience in life, of having to serve the other person, runs totally counter to what their ideas and values were previously. In order to live at peace within themselves, they are forced to drop their previous prejudicial attitudes. They are not able to change their behavior because the cohesiveness of the unit and the dictates of the military will not allow it. So instead of living with an attitude or idea that runs counter to their behavior, over time they will adjust the thinking going on in their minds.

The same thing holds true with loving your enemies. You may not feel like it. You may have justifiable reasons why to not love them. But if you are compelled in anyway to obey the commands of Jesus to be loving towards them, then eventually your attitude will change. You will not be able to keep the kind actions and feelings of hatred alongside one another. In this case the feelings of loving your enemy will follow the actions of love you exhibit towards them. You will be changed to become more and more like Jesus.

But in many cases your enemy will also be changed. You see, they will in all probability also experience some sense of cognitive dissonance. The attitude they previously had towards you will be challenged by their more recent experience with you. The more you act towards them in a loving manner, as Jesus commanded, the more dissonance they will experience and the more they will wrestle with the need to resolve it. In many cases that resolution will come through reconciliation with you. It will happen because they will be confused by your highly unusual reaction to them. People are not used to an enemy treating them with dignity. What they fully expect is to be treated badly in return and thus be able to further justify their terrible opinion of their enemy. An enemy who responds by serving them with Christ-like love just doesn't fit their grid. The question of your motivation then opens the door to pointing to Jesus who performed the ultimate act of love for His enemies. The reconciliation with you is the first step in bringing them into reconciliation with Jesus.

Bringing people into a reconciled relationship with Jesus is the ultimate purpose of acting towards them in a loving way. It goes back to the very beginning, and us being made in the image of God. We represent God to the world. As followers of Christ we represent Him as His ambassadors who have been given the ministry of reconciliation.

"That is, in Christ God was reconciling the world to himself, not counting their trespasses against them, and entrusting to us the message of reconciliation. Therefore, we are ambassadors for Christ, God making his appeal through us. We implore you on behalf of Christ, be reconciled to God" (2 Corinthians 5:19-20).

There are many times I wonder why God didn't have a better plan than relying on us to be His ambassadors who love our enemies and bring them into a relationship with Christ. But when I see how love for our enemies has the ability to totally disarm them, because they expect the opposite from sinful, fellow human beings, then I can appreciate the genius of God's plan. It is precisely because our experience and expectations are the exact opposite that loving our enemies is the most powerful of all testimonies we can make to the power of the gospel.

CHAPTER 14

LOVE GOD, HATE YOUR PARENTS

" 'If anyone comes to me and does not hate his own father and mother and wife and children and brothers and sisters, yes, and even his own life, he cannot be my disciple.' " — Luke 14:26

"You shall have no other gods before me. .... Honor your father and your mother, that your days may be long in the land that the Lord your God is giving you." —Exodus 20: 3, 12

WHAT IN THE WORLD are we supposed to make of Jesus' provocative statement that we are to hate our parents? We have just seen that Jesus wants us to love our enemies. That sounds crazy enough. Now telling us to hate our families and love Jesus makes God out to be some sort of schizophrenic sadist. Could these words possibly come from Jesus and, if so, what in the world do they mean? It seems to be a fairly straightforward statement but does Jesus really want us to hate our families?

When I was a new Christian there was a group that made this verse one of the foundations of their ministry. They sprang up in the late sixties and seventies. It was a time when lots of teenagers were caught up in a spirit of rebellion against any and all authority. This group, known as The Children of God, convinced thousands of young people to renounce their parents, family, and friends and run off to join them. They said it was the only way to really be committed to Jesus. Most people intuitively sensed that this was not what Jesus had in mind but at the same time they didn't know how to respond to what seemed to be a very cut-and-dried understanding of His words. As a result lots of folks simply dismissed these words as something they just didn't understand, and they instead moved on to more familiar, safe verses about how much God loved them. That, by the way, is what we normally do with those parts of God's Word that make us uncomfortable. We put them in a mental box, locked away from any consideration, while we move on to our favorite memory verses that make us feel good about ourselves and Jesus.

But we can't just ignore what Jesus said because it makes us uncomfortable, especially when He seems so intent on provoking some kind of reaction in us. He says these hard things with the intent of forcing us to wrestle with them and be shaped by them in ways we would normally work hard to avoid. The enemy, Satan, would like nothing more than for us to blow off such provocative verses and refuse to get any deeper in our faith than having some vague sense that God thinks we are OK and that the Bible is just too hard to understand. It is not so hard to understand—it is hard to accept and believe. There is a difference.

We need to wrestle with what Jesus meant. We have already seen that He is God come in the flesh, and that He is indeed the Lord. That means the only reasonable thing to do is try to understand what He meant and what it requires of us to follow Him. In order to understand what Jesus meant it will be helpful to first understand what He did not mean. Clearly, Jesus would not teach that we are to hate anyone in the way that we normally think of hatred. After all, it was Jesus who commanded that we not even hate our enemies but instead we love them. It was also Jesus who said the two most important things you could do were to love God with all your heart, mind, soul, and strength, and love your neighbor as yourself. Surely we are not expected to love our neighbor as we love ourselves and at the same time detest our parent and siblings.

Some people try to use this as an example of a contradiction in the Bible and an excuse to ignore all of it. But there is no contradiction. Jesus doesn't speak out of both sides of His mouth, at one time saying love your enemies and the next despise and detest your parents. When Jesus says to hate your parents He uses the Greek word, *miseo*. It is a word that has dual usage. It can mean to despise or detest someone, but it is also used in the Bible and other ancient literature to mean "love less."

Numerous scholars of the Bible concur that in this and many other cases *miseo* is used to mean love one thing less than another. It is a matter of placing higher priority over one thing than another.

With that in mind the meaning of Jesus becomes easy to grasp but harder to live. What Jesus is saying is that there should be nothing in this world that we love more than we love Him. We are not to love our parents more than we love Jesus. We are not to love our brothers and sisters more than we love Jesus. We are not to love our children, or spouse, or cousins, or next-door neighbor more than we love Jesus. In fact, He says that we are not to love our own life more than we love Jesus.

That shouldn't surprise us for two reasons. First, God said in the Ten Commandments that we are to have no other gods before Him. In other words, nothing in life is to have more devotion from us than the Lord our God. Second, Jesus said that we are to love God with all that we have and all that we are. The implication is simple: nothing and no one should have a greater place in our heart, and in our devotion, and in our love, than the Lord.

Raising three boys has been one of the most satisfying experiences of my life. My sons know that I love them unconditionally and will serve them in any way I can. They know that no one outside our family will ever be more important to me than they are. But they also know that if push comes to shove they take a back seat to their mom, my wife. There was once an issue that Zack, our oldest, had with Barb. I don't remember the details, but I do remember the conversation. It was an attempt on his part to get me on his side in a dispute he was having with his mother. I think I even somewhat agreed with him. But I also remember that it was an issue that was very important to Barb, and she was not going to budge. My response to Zack was simple. "Son, I can't help you out on this one," I told him. "One day you are going to move out on your own, have your own job and family. On occasion you will come home for a visit to your mom and me. I, however, have to live with her for the rest of my days. Sorry son, you lose." Now, I said all of that with a bit of a smile on my face, and he was bright enough to understand what I meant. That doesn't mean he wasn't still frustrated in not getting it his way. However, he still knew that Barb and I had always told him and his brothers: We loved God first, then one another, and then them as our sons. Being third in that list did not mean that we did not love them. It certainly did not mean that we hated them. It just meant that the relationship with God came first, our relationship as husband and wife came second, and that our relationship with them came third. On a scale of comparison our love for them was *miseo*. We loved them less than we loved God.

I am sure that some people reading this will be perplexed, uncomfortable, or even outright indignant that we would let our children think that we did not love them as much as we possibly could. But that would be a wrong assumption. You see, by putting God first in our love priority list, even above loving each other as husband and wife, and above loving our children, we were loving our children as much as we possibly could. We were being more loving towards them by placing them behind God in the loving priority than we could ever possibly love them otherwise. Let me put it this way: by loving God more than anything else, we were able to love our children more than we ever could.

If, in fact, God is love and the source of all love, then the more I love Him the more my capacity to love others will grow. It is not as if by loving God more than anyone or anything else that I am somehow going to shortchange those other objects of my affection. Exactly the opposite is true. As I learn to love God more deeply, I learn more of what it means to truly love and be loved. By giving of myself in love to my creator and redeemer, I receive far more than I give. I receive a greater capacity to love others. The more I love God, the more I receive, the more my capacity to love others increases, the more I can give love to them. If I were to love my parents, my wife, or my children more than I love God, then over time I would end up shortchanging all of them. My human capacity to love is limited by my frailty and sin. When I love God less than something or someone else, then I am drawing on my own limited capacity to love and that capacity will eventually, most likely quickly, be drained. But when I put God as my first love, then my capacity for loving others becomes immeasurable.

To emphasize the fact that we are to love nothing so much as we love the Lord, Jesus goes on in Luke 14:27 and says, "And anyone who does not carry his cross and follow me cannot be my disciple." The folks who heard those words come from His mouth had to have been stunned to the point of being frozen in their tracks. The image of carrying a cross was vivid to them. Anytime someone was carrying a cross they were on their way to their own execution. They were going to death, just as Jesus was when He carried His own cross. By saying that we are to love Jesus more than we love our parents and that we are to carry our cross for Him or else we are unworthy of being His disciples, Jesus is saying that when it comes to following Him, He wants our all. There is no halfway measure with Jesus. It is full and complete de-votion or nothing. It is Jesus first or not at all. It is give Him your life even to the point of death, or not at all.

Sometimes your love for the Lord might mean that you have to say no to your family and yes to Jesus. Sometimes your love for the Lord might mean that you have to turn down a promo-tion, because even though it will mean more money and pres-tige you know that it will have a negative impact on your rela-tionship with Jesus. Sometimes your love for the Lord might mean that you must sacrifice your comfort and open your home to someone with nowhere to live. Sometimes your love for the Lord means you must live with rejection from people whom you care about, or face ridicule from others. You must love them and their acceptance and your comfort and your promotion and your prestige less than you love Jesus.

So the right thing to say is not, "Mom and Dad, I love Jesus but I hate you." Instead, it needs to be, "Mom and Dad and anyone or anything else, I love you, but I love Jesus most of all."

Chapter 15

LET STRANGERS LIVE IN YOUR HOUSE

"Do not neglect to show hospitality to strangers, for thereby some have entertained angels unawares." — Hebrews 13:2

"Let love be genuine. Abhor what is evil; hold fast to what is good. Love one another with brotherly affection. Outdo one another in showing honor. Do not be slothful in zeal, be fervent in spirit, serve the Lord. Rejoice in hope, be patient in tribulation, be constant in prayer. Contribute to the needs of the saints and seek to show hospitality." — Romans 12:9-13

"Hospitality should have no other nature than love." — Henrietta Mears

ONE OF THE MOST common practices in the early church was that of hospitality. It was radical hospitality. It started with Jesus never having a house of His own and most often staying in homes of people who demonstrated radical hospitality. It continued when He sent out the first disciples, telling them to preach the Good News and to stay in the homes of people who would offer them a bed. It culminated in the letter to the Hebrews, in which the author urges radical hospitality for a radical reason:

"Do not neglect to show hospitality to strangers, for thereby some have entertained angels unawares" (Hebrews 13:2).

What an amazing statement! The writer is saying that some people have actually opened their homes to angels without knowing it. How incredible! Movies and television programs are full of the theme of angels stepping into the world and making an impact without us even knowing it. Movies like *It's a Wonderful Life* and *Angels in the Outfield*, and programs like *Touched by an Angel* all revolve around angels in our midst. But the writer to the Hebrews is not talking about fantasy. He is talking about real life.

It is mind-blowing to think that people could put a sign outside their house saying that "An Angel Slept Here." But what is more amazing to me is that there were probably some people who missed the opportunity by actually turning a stranger away. If people showed hospitality to angels without knowing it, then certainly people turned away angels without knowing it. What a missed opportunity that must have been.

The move away from any kind of hospitality to a culture in which we hide behind our walls and separate ourselves from others is well documented. How often does the typical suburbanite drive home from work, hit the garage door remote, pull into the garage, close the garage door with the push of a button from inside the car, and walk into the house without ever engaging his or her neighbors? Most people don't even know their neighbors' names. What a radical shift it would be if Christians actually started inviting their neighbors over for a barbecue or Super Bowl party. But that stuff is not even close to being radical. That's just being a nice neighbor.

The early church was radical. Paul could travel anywhere there were Christians and always have a place to stay. It was so common for Christians to open their homes to others that at the turn of the first century there were already written-down standards for such things. It was considered a privilege to open your home to people. Today we only see the extra work and burden of it all.

When I look at our family I can see that we have practiced some radical hospitality, but we pale in comparison to those first generations of Christians. This past Christmas we opened our home for a week to two students from Taiwan whom we had never met before. They were not Christians but we had some great conversations about God. The best part was that they started the conversations by asking questions. An added blessing was that my youngest son, Garrett, got to practice his Mandarin with them and build an ongoing relationship. A few months earlier we had three men from Zambia stay with us. Again, we had never met them before, but we provided a home for them for a few days. In that case it was so they could be part of a choir raising money to support a school in their hometown in Africa. There are more such stories I could share, but the point you would get from all of them is that every time we have opened our home to others we have been blessed far beyond what we sacrificed.

The most common objection people give to opening their home to strangers is a fear for the safety of the family. Yet, if we really pray and seek God in this we should not fear. I have a friend in South Africa who opened his home to a man who was just released from prison. This man was on parole having spent years in jail on a murder charge. My friend and his wife opened their home and as a result they are being used by God to change this man's life. That is the kind of hospitality God wants us to demonstrate because that is provocative and changes lives for His glory.

THE POWER OF HOSPITALITY

Aside from the obvious practical benefits of first-century hospitality, making missions possible, and the blessing received by those who show hospitality, there is a further and more powerful reason why God places such an emphasis on this ministry. It has to do with the dignity and equality that is bestowed when we show hospitality.

There was a serious religious, racial, and economic division in the early church. Jews historically refused to eat with Gentiles or even enter their homes out of fear of being spiritually contaminated. The rich wanted nothing to do with sharing a meal with the poor, and Romans and Greeks looked down on one another with equal disdain. Christian hospitality served the vital purpose of breaking down those barriers and demonstrating that all who are in Christ are one body and stand equal at the foot of the cross.

How does hospitality do this? It has to do with the intimacy of hospitality and of sharing a meal together. When you open your home to someone, you are opening your life to them, your world. You are risking letting them know who you really are. Taking that risk says to the other person, "I value you enough to let you into my world and to serve you." It lets them know that you see them as a person of worth, and equal before Christ.

Sharing a meal together adds to that dignity or intimacy. In most Western cultures sharing a meal has lost something of its social, personal intimacy. Fewer and fewer people have family meals together, not to mention meals with guests. Meals are often eaten on the run or in front of a television screen. Additionally there is really very little sharing of food. I contrast that with meals I have shared with others in different cultures. Ethiopians, for example, share food from common bowls. But don't get the idea that it is American family-style, where you have big serving spoons and take the mashed potatoes from a bowl using them, putting the food onto your plate from which you take it using your own fork. No. You reach in with your hand to the common bowl to get whatever food you are going to eat and take it directly to your mouth. The person next to you does the same thing. But the intimacy goes beyond that. They have a practice called *goorsha*, the sharing of the bread together. You not only eat from the same bowl by dipping your piece of bread, you also eat from the same bread that was dipped. Think about the Last Supper, when Jesus mentioned that the one who would betray Him was the one with whom His hand dipped the bread in the bowl. This is common practice for Ethiopians. They are used to the intimacy of dipping together in the same dish and whenever they read about Jesus and Judas it reminds them of their own practice. Now, if you get crazy when someone double-dips a chip in the salsa, then this will put you over the edge. It is like sharing the same spoon with the person next to you. You cannot and will not do that unless there is a nearly supernatural acceptance of the person you are eating with.

When I was a boy, my best friend was Bobby Kramer. How do I know he was my best friend? Simple: Bobby and I could drink out of the same Coke bottle without wiping the top first! I know, it sounds incredibly unclean in this day and age, but that's how it was. Such an act said, "You are not unclean, you are my equal." The same thing is being said when you eat with Ethiopians. The refusal of Jews to eat with Gentiles said the opposite. It said, "You are unclean, and you are beneath me."

So does it work? Do people really feel that you confer dignity on them by opening your life and home to them? You bet. Let me give you just one example.

A few years ago, my wife and I had the privilege of opening our home to a pastor and his wife from South Africa. They were with us for almost two weeks and it was a delight for us to host them. Little did we know the impact our hospitality would have on them and us. The pastor's wife had never stayed in the home of a white person before. In fact, I am fairly certain that she had never stepped inside a white person's home. It was her choice to avoid that. For years the system of apartheid in South Africa was used to keep blacks oppressed and virtually enslaved. Her bitterness toward the whites who promoted such a system had led her to make a decision to stay as far away from them as possible.

During their stay with Barb and me, we had breakfast together around our table most every morning, as well as dinner. The conversations sometimes lasted for hours, covering everything from politics and economics to children and ministry. On the final night together we were in the middle of another meal and great conversation when the wife put her knife and fork on the table and said very seriously, "I have a speech to make." Clearly this was important, so Barb and I also put down our utensils and gave her our full attention.

Our guest proceeded to let us know that she had not been in favor of staying in our home, but that her husband had convinced her that they needed to do this. As a result of staying with us, her perspective on white people was beginning to change. She said she had made a point of watching us to see if we were real or not. People could be nice for a short period of time, she knew, but we had loved them the entire time they were with us, she said. We had served her and her husband, treated them as true brother and sister in Christ, opened our home and our lives to them, and as a result God was changing her.

That is why hospitality is so important in our world today. It confers dignity, respect, and honor. It confers grace on people. That is what hospitality is all about. It is about giving people grace. The best compliment you can give a hostess is not how great the food was, or how beautiful the centerpiece was, or how lovely the house is. The greatest compliment you can give a host is that they were gracious. In being gracious they put the focus on serving and honoring the guest, not on their own ability to entertain, cook, or decorate.

Jesus was the ultimate host. His first act of ministry in John 1 was to invite some young men to come and be where He was staying. His final corporate act before the crucifixion was to invite people to share a meal that He hosted. One day He will invite all who have believed and trusted in Him to share a great banquet feast around His heavenly table. At that feast He will confer upon us the dignity and honor of being eternal sons and daughters of God.

CHAPTER 16

BLESSED ARE YOU WHEN PEOPLE HATE YOU

" 'Blessed are you when others revile you and persecute you and utter all kinds of evil against you falsely on my account.' " — Matthew 5:11

" 'A disciple is not above his teacher, nor a servant above his master. It is enough for the disciple to be like his teacher, and the servant like his master. If they have called the master of the house Beelzebul, how much more will they malign those of his household. So have no fear of them, for nothing is covered that will not be revealed, or hidden that will not be known.' " — Matthew 10:24-26

"If you live in such a manner as to stand the test of the last judgment, you can depend upon it that the world will not speak well of you." — Alistair Begg

"Be of good comfort, Mr. Ridley, and play the man! We shall this day light such a candle by God's grace, in England, as I trust never shall be put out." — Hugh Latimer (as he was burned at the stake with Nicholas Ridley in Oxford, England, in 1555)

DON'T PARTICULARLY ENJOY having people mad at me, and I certainly don't like having people hate me. There is something in me that feels like I have failed if that happens. I must have said something wrong, sinned against them in some way. Maybe I didn't express myself clearly and need to rephrase something. Most times I probably spoke in haste and said something I should not have said. It bothers me when that happens to the point that I feel compelled to rush out and fix it, as well as to try once again to fix whatever it is in me that caused the problem. Having people hate me just feels all wrong and twisted.

But I have come to realize that sometimes having people hate you is actually a good thing. It has been said that the kind of person you are is revealed as much by those who are counted among your friends as those who are counted among your enemies. That is certainly the case when it comes to Jesus. His friends were the outcasts, tax collectors, drunkards, prostitutes, lepers, and lots of everyday common working stiffs. His enemies were the outwardly pious who were inwardly protecting their power, influence, and wealth. They were the ones who would eventually plot and carry out His execution.

Why were they His enemies? The answer lies in the fact that Jesus challenged their carefully constructed world. He challenged their notions of themselves and God. He challenged their position, their power, and their pride. He did it by speaking the truth, and sometimes speaking the truth results in people hating you, especially if it is a painful truth.

Jesus made it clear that if we follow in His footsteps and speak the truth and live a life of radical devotion to God, then there will be times when we will be hated, reviled, and persecuted. If it happened to Him, the master and leader, then how much more likely is it to happen to His lowly followers? Because a disciple is not above her master, she should not expect to be treated better than the master; in fact, she should expect to be treated more harshly and with greater disdain.

"OK, so I get it that people will hate me because of my relationship with Jesus. But how does that translate into a blessing?" It certainly doesn't feel very positive when that happens, and it is difficult to see what benefit we gain when people hate us.

When we speak of blessing, especially as it is used in the New Testament, it most often refers to our relationship with God. Being blessed points to the deep abiding joy that can only come from knowing that God smiles upon us and that we are in a relationship with Him that cannot be broken. The relationship experienced by a follower of Jesus is one that carries with it a sense of belonging, being connected, valued, and loved by God that from the depths of your being gives you peace and joy and contentment. In his letter to the Ephesians, Paul puts it this way: *"Blessed be the God and Father of our Lord Jesus Christ, who has blessed us in Christ with every spiritual blessing in the heavenly places"* (Ephesians 1:3).

We were made to be in relationship with God. That is evident from the opening chapters of Genesis, and has been explored already in the early chapters of this book. We also saw that our relationship with God was severely damaged when we rebelled against God through sin. In a sense, a spiritual and even a physical wall was erected between God and us because of sin. What didn't change was the basic hard-wired need we have to be connected to Him. Nothing could be a greater blessing than to have that relationship restored. The promises of heaven that the Bible gives us are filled with the assurance of being once again in that relationship, unencumbered by our sin. The blessings that the New Testament speaks of are blessings that affirm that relationship and assure us of the eventual fulfillment of God's promise that He will redeem all creation and those who love and trust Jesus Christ.

When we suffer persecution because we are followers of Christ we are blessed, in the very least because such persecution is a tangible if painful assurance that we belong to Christ in this life and will also belong to Him in the life to come. There is something of this to be found in Acts 7, where the Sanhedrin, the Jewish high council, arrested a group of the apostles. These were the same people who had arrested and crucified Jesus not long before. After much debate it was determined that it would be a bad idea to punish the apostles. But the council just couldn't bring themselves to let the apostles walk away unscathed. So they had them beaten and ordered them to stop preaching about Jesus.

You would think after seeing what Jesus went through in being crucified, and getting beaten severely for preaching about Him, that the apostles might have had at least a moment of reconsideration about their fate. Instead, they were emboldened all the more. Acts 5:41-42 tells us that after the beating and warning: *"Then they left the presence of the council, rejoicing that they were counted worthy to suffer dishonor for the name. And every day, in the temple and from house to house, they did not cease teaching and preaching that the Christ is Jesus."*

Not only did they continue to preach that Jesus was the Christ, the Messiah, incredibly they rejoiced over the beating they received.

Now don't get the idea that these were some kind of religious masochists. They didn't go looking for a beating. But when it came their way they considered it akin to a badge of honor. They were honored to be worthy enough to be persecuted for Jesus' name. For those apostles there was a blessing in the beating. It meant to them that they really were following Jesus as they ought. It meant that they were identified as belonging to Jesus. I am certain that in their minds they had thoughts of what Jesus went through on their behalf and this was a small price to pay to be identified with Him. They rejoiced! Blessing from God does that. It gives you a deep and satisfying joy because of your relationship to Him. The apostles' suffering showed they would stand with and for Jesus no matter what. They would have ample opportunity to prove that again and again, as all but one of them would eventually suffer a martyr's death for Christ.

In the midst of those sufferings the apostles never doubted that they were blessed. That is only possible if your focus is on the spiritual side of blessing and not strictly on blessings of comfort, prosperity, and abundance. Certainly the Bible points to physical and material blessings that can be had from the hand of God. But that is only one aspect of biblical blessing. Unfortunately it is the most desired and focused on aspect of blessing, while being the least important and meaningful.

Throughout Christianity there is a growing theology of blessing that focuses on material and physical prosperity as the only true signs that God favors you and that you have faith. The name, "the prosperity gospel," should in and of itself tell you something is wrong with the theology behind it. Anytime you need to put an adjective in front of "gospel" to define your gospel you are treading on thin ice. The gospel is what it is and adjectives that describe it as "prosperity," "American," "Peter's," or any other word run the risk of turning it into something other than the gospel of Jesus and the New Testament.

One of the dangers of the prosperity gospel is that it views hardship and suffering as sure signs that you are lacking faith, or are in some way out of favor with God. His blessing is not on you if you are not healthy, rich, comfortable and powerful. But think about that for just a moment. What requires more faith—to follow God when you are rich and healthy, or when you are being beaten and an outcast? It is the same question Satan posed to God in the beginning of the book of Job, who would have been the poster child for the prosperity gospel in his day.

God rightly delights in Job's faithfulness, but Satan rebuts that "of course Job trusts you. His life is perfect. Let a little hardship come his way and see what happens."

Job eventually learns to trust God no matter what happens. In his encounter with God he finds a deeper understanding of who he is and who God is. It is a priceless blessing that could only have come in the hardships of life. That is true of all hardship, including persecution. When you are reviled and berated for your faith in Jesus and you cling to Him more closely, then you receive blessings that only come in the midst of such struggle. Being identified with Jesus through persecution is something that the early church understood. They didn't question if Jesus had abandoned them. It was quite the opposite; they saw the persecution as evidence that they were drawing closer to Christ.

That is what the apostles experienced in Acts 7. They had a deep, abiding joy in the midst of their persecution because it identified them more closely with Jesus. Their focus and priority was not on this life and the possibility of living what we would call the American dream. Life, liberty, and the pursuit of happiness were not their highest goals or ideals. The comforts and blessings of health and financial prosperity were not their goal. Heaven was their goal. Living in such a way as to honor Christ in everything before getting there was their goal. The blessing of being counted worthy of the name by which they were called was their goal. Persecution only served to tell them that they were on the right path. Just as Jesus, for the joy set before Him, endured the cross (Hebrews 12:2), those early followers endured persecution and rejection as a blessing from God.

Chapter 17

Forgive, Again and Again and Again and...

"Be kind to one another, tenderhearted, forgiving one another, as God in Christ forgave you." — Ephesians 4:32

"Then Peter came up and said to him, 'Lord, how often will my brother sin against me, and I forgive him? As many as seven times?' Jesus said to him, 'I do not say to you seven times, but seventy-seven times.' "
— Matthew 18:21-22

"The weak can never forgive. Forgiveness is the attribute of the strong."
— Mahatma Gandhi

"Forgiveness is me giving up my right to hurt you for hurting me."
— Anonymous

HOW MANY TIMES HAVE you heard the statement, "I can forgive, but I can't forget"? When I hear those words they are nearly always spoken with a tone that says, "I am holding onto the pain and I will deal with the offender accordingly." What seems to be said is, "I forgive, therefore I will not seek revenge, even though I could. But I will treat this person differently as a result of their offense." If I am right and that is what often lies behind the statement, then we really do not understand the nature of forgiveness or forgetting.

If you are to truly forgive someone, then you must never forget what they have done. Yes, you read that right. If you are to truly forgive someone, then you must never forget what they have done. If you forget it, then you have not forgiven. The point of forgiveness is to treat someone with love and respect even when you do remember how they have hurt you.

Let's look at an encounter between Jesus and Peter following the resurrection to understand this. During the Last Supper Jesus predicted that the disciples would all abandon Him in the coming hours. Peter, ever the bold one, objected vociferously, saying that all the others might abandon Jesus but he never would. At that point Jesus specifically told Peter that before the cock crowed Peter would deny three times ever knowing Him. Sure enough that is exactly what happened. But it was even more painful than that. Look at the description of that denial in Luke 22:54-62:

"Then they seized him and led him away, bringing him into the high priest's house, and Peter was following at a distance. And when they had kindled a fire in the middle of the courtyard and sat down together, Peter sat down among them. Then a servant girl, seeing him as he sat in the light and looking closely at him, said, 'This man also was with him.' But he denied it, saying, 'Woman, I do not know him.' And a little later someone else saw him and said, 'You also are one of them.' But Peter said, 'Man, I am not.' And after an interval of about an hour still another insisted, saying, 'Certainly this man also was with him, for he too is a Galilean.' But Peter said, 'Man, I do not know what you are talking about.' And immediately, while he was still speaking, the rooster crowed. And the Lord turned and looked at Peter. And Peter remembered the saying of the Lord, how he had said to him, 'Before the rooster crows today, you will deny me three times.' And he went out and wept bitterly."

Did you notice the incredibly important detail in the last sentence? Immediately after Peter's third denial of Jesus the rooster crows and Jesus, on trial for His life, looks across the courtyard and locks eyes with Peter. Put yourself in Peter's sandals for a moment and try to imagine the shame and guilt that flood you. Imagine yourself now, if you can, in Jesus' sandals and imagine the broken-heartedness of betrayal but also the heart that is broken for Peter because you know the pain that he is experiencing as never before, and because you love him you heart aches for him.

Wonderfully, a few days after the crucifixion, Jesus rises from the dead. Peter and John race to the tomb, hoping against hope that the report from the women of an empty tomb is true. It is! Over the next few weeks there are many encounters between Jesus and His followers, but none more poignant than that between Jesus and Peter in John 21. Jesus asks Peter three times, "Do you love me?" At the third asking, Peter is heartbroken. Why? Because the last time Peter was asked the same question three times he denied even knowing Jesus. Jesus knows that and remembers that. Remember the locked eyes across the courtyard. You can be certain that image was burned into both their brains. In an incredible act of grace Jesus puts that event back on the table and lets Peter know that it is all right; he is forgiven and restored.

In order to truly forgive Peter, Jesus had to remember the betrayal. Then, in spite of the pain that the betrayal gave Him, Jesus treats Peter as a brother whom He loves and has forgiven.

Forgiveness is about treating someone with the love of God in spite of what they have done. When you remember the pain of rejection, the anguish of betrayal, the shock of being sinned against, forgiveness becomes evident when you still treat that other person like Jesus treated Peter—like He treats you. If I never remember what they have done, I am not being forgiving. I am just absent-minded.

Forgiving and remembering means that not only do I refuse to take revenge but I also determine to do something positive.

I determine to treat you with love, respect, and dignity and I will not hold your sin against you. That sounds an awful lot like the way God treats us because of Jesus Christ and His death on the cross.

In October 2006, thirty-two-year-old Charlie Roberts entered a small, all-girls Amish schoolhouse in Lancaster County, Pennsylvania. Once inside he shot and killed five young girls, wounded five others, and eventually killed himself. In a tight-knit community like the Amish, everyone was tragically devastated by the shootings. No one was left untouched, including Charlie's mother, Terri Roberts. How could she possibly continue to live in that community knowing that her son had murdered five little girls and seriously wounded five others?

Her answer came before the sun rose on another day. The people of that community, following the Lord's command to forgive and love your neighbor, descended on the Roberts' home and expressed their love and forgiveness. The very first people who went to Terri were a mother and father whose daughters were two of the five who had been murdered. They prayed for Terri and asked her to not leave the community, but stay. In the midst of their own pain the people of that community knew that there was another victim, and it was Terri Roberts. They understood the shame and guilt that she would feel, and they knew that they and only they had the power to remove that shame and guilt and her healing. That power was the power of forgiveness.

Terri Roberts is still in that community, and actually serves as a caregiver to one of the most seriously-wounded girls. She has found a purpose in the pain. It doesn't remove the pain entirely but she doesn't wallow in it and is not overcome by it. The same can be said of the people in the community, especially those whose daughters were shot. The pain never entirely goes away, but in the midst of it there is hope. It is there only because some people took the difficult step of obedience to follow Jesus into forgiveness.

One of the amazing aspects of forgiveness that we see in this story is the power of forgiveness to help people rebuild their broken lives. What would Terri Roberts' life have been like if she hadn't received that forgiveness from the community? What would Peter's life be like if Jesus had not directly confronted the issue and welcomed him back into the fold? Forgiveness is a powerful tool in the hand of God, and He puts it in our hands to change lives forever.

It is important that the person whom we are to forgive knows that we know and that we remember what they did. It cannot be left to just forgetting about it and moving on. Without the act of actually walking up the front steps of Terri Roberts' house and expressing forgiveness, there would always have been a pall hanging over her life, even if people in the community were civil as they met on the street. She needed the power of that painful encounter and needed to hear that she was forgiven. If Jesus had never brought Peter's denials to the table, yet treated him well, there would have always been a lingering doubt. Peter would never have really known if he was forgiven, or if Jesus simply forgot about the denials or was too polite or uncomfortable to bring them up. He, like Terri Roberts, would have been eaten alive by guilt and doubt. But by putting it all out in the open, Jesus and the Amish community made it clear that they knew what was done and yet they still loved and forgave. Forgiving and forgetting is not the answer. Remembering and forgiving is the answer.

All of this focuses on the power of forgiveness in the life of the offender. But there is an equally compelling reason for the need of forgiveness in the life of the offended. Think about that Amish community. If they had not gone to Terri Roberts and offered her the love and forgiveness that can only come through Christ, not only would Terri have had to live forever under the painful weight of that October day, so would everyone else in the community. All their lives would be forever stuck on that day. The pain and sorrow still remain; they never completely leave after a tragedy like that. But they are differ-ent when forgiveness is offered and love is practiced. The pain lessens. There is a hope that slowly pokes its way up out of the muck and mire of the tragedy and eventually points to a future that holds some promise. The people of that community have experienced that, as have countless others who have learned to forgive even as they remember. They will never forget their little girls or how they died. But because they are able to for-give they are not incapacitated by the grief. Rather they have a purpose in it—to demonstrate the power of Christ and bring glory to Him as they give Christ-like forgiveness to another.

Our failure to forgive others keeps us in bondage. When you fail to take the hard road of learning to love your neighbor, or your enemy, or the one who painfully wronged you, you will find yourself forever stuck in a pit that from time to time over-whelms you. Forgiveness is hard in the short term. But stay-ing stuck in the pit of unforgiveness, while easier in the short term, is death in the long term.

Where do you find the power to get out of the pit and for-give? It comes from what Paul says in Ephesians 4:32: *"Be kind to one another, tenderhearted, forgiving one another, as God in Christ forgave you."* The only way I am able to forgive anoth-er person is to remind myself daily of the forgiveness I have in Christ. I am compelled to forgive another, who is really my equal, fellow human being, because I have been forgiven by Christ, the Lord of lords and King of kings. I cannot and must not withhold from my equal what has been freely given to me by He who is my superior in every conceivable way.

That is the point of Jesus' parable of the unforgiving servant, in Matthew 18. He tells that story immediately following the disciples' question about how often they need to forgive. Their goal is seven times. Jesus makes it seventy times seven. That is not to be taken as 490 times but, as has already been pointed out, it means again and again. To drive home the point Jesus then tells of a servant who was forgiven a huge debt by his master only to turn around and refuse to forgive a fellow servant a miniscule debt and have his fellow servant tossed into a debtor's prison. Upon hearing of this injustice the master immediately throws the unforgiving servant in prison, saying that he had been forgiven a huge debt by the master and should have therefore understood and been compelled to forgive a small debt by an equal.

By comparison, any offense against us—even the murder of a daughter, as hard as it may be to grasp—is small compared to the debt we owe our Lord God because of our sin and rebellion against Him. Forgiveness is not an option. It is a necessity. It is necessary for the one who has offended us, but it is equally if not more necessary for us to forgive when we are offended.

Chapter 18

TURN THE OTHER CHEEK

" 'But I say to you, Do not resist the one who is evil. But if anyone slaps you on the right cheek, turn to him the other also.' " — Matthew 5:39

"I began imagining scenes in public which some drunk would come up to me and slap me in the face. Nothing like that ever happened, but I often wonder if I would have turned the other cheek." — Max von Sydow

"In taking revenge, a man is but even with his enemy; but in passing it over, he is superior." — Francis Bacon

MANY PEOPLE WANT TO ignore Jesus' provocative words in Matthew 5:39 because they seem to imply that we are to allow people to just beat the tar out of us, and not resist physical violence and injury. Having a sense of what I think Jesus really meant by these words causes me to wonder at how easily we get deceived into believing that it means something that is impossible to obey. God does not give us commands that are impossible to obey. He certainly gives us ones that are difficult and that challenge us, but never ones that are impossible.

To understand what God wants of us, it is important to catch key details. Anytime the Bible gives a particularly vivid detail we need to pay attention. There is one in this verse that speaks volumes. Jesus said that if someone "strikes you on the right cheek," then you are to turn your face to him in such a way as to present your left cheek—the implication being that he may hit you again. What is the significance of the "right" cheek?

Why not the left one? Picture someone getting hit on the right cheek: What is the most likely way for that to happen? Since most people are right-handed and would hit someone with their right hand, then the only way for them to hit someone on the person's right cheek is to do it as a backhanded slap. What Jesus is speaking about here is not letting someone pummel you into a pile of broken bones. Rather, He is talking about taking an insult. A backhanded slap is just that. It is an insult that challenges you to retaliate. It is an attempt to shame you and get you to either back down in utter humiliation or lash out and escalate the conflict.

To turn the other cheek is neither humiliating nor retaliation. It is rather a response of strength that says, "I will not seek revenge because I am stronger than that." It also says, "I will not respond in shame because I have dignity in Christ. My dignity is not found in whether I can hit you back and hurt you. My dignity is found in Christ and I will respond in just the way He would respond."

In practice there are very few times in one's life when another person would give you an actual backhanded slap. There are times when they might give you a verbal one, or show great disrespect for you in some other way. It is those things that get people all worked up and excited. Think of how often you see people arguing and fighting because someone "disrespected" them. What they are looking for is dignity. They want an acknowledgment that they are a person of substance and importance. If someone does not give them that respect, then they feel somehow violated.

When such violations of our dignity happen there is a natural desire to do something to regain our respect and dignity. The means to regain them is far too often to exert power over the other person and show that you are stronger, better, more significant than they are. So instead of turning the other cheek, we strike back. But the retaliation is never equal. It is never a returned backhand slap on the cheek. It is always a matter of escalation. It is an age-old tactic, going back as far as the early chapters of Genesis. In Genesis 4 we get a list of the descendants of Cain. One of them is named Lamech, and he has definite issues with his dignity being besmirched:

"Lamech said to his wives: 'Adah and Zillah, hear my voice; you wives of Lamech, listen to what I say: I have killed a man for wounding me, a young man for striking me. If Cain's revenge is sevenfold, then Lamech's is seventy-sevenfold.'" (Genesis 4:23-24).

Do you see the escalation? A man wounded him, so he killed that man. He boasts about it as part of his manly prowess. He goes on to promise that if Cain is to be revenged seven times over—referring back to a promise from God that He would not allow Cain to be pursued and attacked out of revenge for the death of Abel—then Lamech vows that he himself will take revenge on someone with seventy-seven times the force and power brought against him. This is escalation in the extreme. It is intended by Lamech to show that he is the biggest man on campus. He is eleven times more significant than his ancestor Cain, and far more significant than any other man who would ever dare cross him or his path.

The Bible tells us of Lamech, not as a role model to follow in order to maintain our dignity, but rather as a pathetic character with no sense of where his dignity and significance comes from. He thinks it is all about power over others. What makes that especially startling is that Genesis 4 is only a few pages removed from Genesis 1, which tells us clearly that our dignity comes from being made in the image of God. We looked at that in the beginning of this book because it serves as a crucial foundational truth about who we are, what our purpose is, and where we are going. Lamech missed all of that completely.

Our dignity comes because we are made in the image of God. Our significance comes because we are called by Jesus to be world-changers. Our power and strength comes because we are filled with the Holy Spirit who gives us the ability to receive the insults of others and respond as Christ responded to those who hurled insults at Him.

Black athletes who broke the color barrier in professional sports understood this. People like Jackie Robinson knew that they would face insult after insult. Those insults were intended to humiliate and incite a response. The hope was that a violent response would then justify the impression of the black man as out of control and uncivilized. But when the response was a quiet dignity that came from within, it changed the world. Racial barriers began to fall and reconciliation started to take place.

It is no different for Christians. When we respond to insults with the same kind of vindictiveness, then we affirm for the world that Christianity is a sham. But when we respond in quiet dignity, drawing on the power of Christ, we provoke a response of respect and wonder, and we compel people to want to learn more about Jesus. Turning the other cheek is not impossible, but it is difficult. But when we do respond with the gentle dignity of Jesus, then we bring glory to Him.

CHAPTER 19

SUBMIT TO ONE ANOTHER

"... submitting to one another out of reverence for Christ." — Ephesians 5:21

"One should respect public opinion insofar as is necessary to avoid starvation and keep out of prison, but anything that goes beyond this is voluntary submission to an unnecessary tyranny." — Bertrand Russell

"True strength lies in submission which permits one to dedicate his life, through devotion, to something beyond himself." — Henry Miller

SINCE THE 1970S ONE of the mainstays of pop psychology has been that in order to be an emotionally healthy human being you absolutely must look out for yourself first. You must make sure that you have strong self-esteem. Most importantly, you must never put yourself in a position of considering others to be more important than yourself. That is seen as degrading and demeaning. You should be strong, positive, stand up for yourself, and rise above the others. In the corporate world that translates into winning by having people serve you, getting the corner office, making people bend to your will. In the marriage relationship it becomes taking care of yourself, making sure that you are being fulfilled.

Certainly the last thing on the minds of pop psychologists and the liberated twenty-first-century human being is that in order to really be fulfilled we should actually submit to others. Yet that is exactly what the Bible teaches, over and over and over again. The wisdom of God is completely counterintuitive. Jesus said that if you want to gain your life, you must lose it. He said that if you want to be the greatest among people, then you must become the servant of all. The Bible says that if we want to truly live, then we must die to ourselves. In Ephesians 5, Paul says that if we want to be truly fulfilled then we need to empty ourselves and submit to one another out of reverence for Christ.

Somehow in our vocabulary "to submit" has come to mean to give up and be the ultimate loser. It means that someone else is dominant and rules over you, and that you have no control of your life. Most recently, being submissive has been defined in terms of "having no voice." It is the image of a person cowering in such fear and humiliation that they can't even speak to defend themselves. What a sad and pitiful definition of a wonderfully powerful and empowering biblical concept.

Mutual submission is not about one person winning and everyone else losing. It is not about having no voice or no power or no control. The reason it is none of these things is because submission as a biblical concept is fulfilled when everyone submits to everyone else because we love Jesus. Submission is never a one-way street. Paul tells wives why and how to submit to their husbands. But he also tells husbands why and how to submit to their wives, and children to parents and even parents to children.

You see, what Jesus wants to see happen is that we never have to worry about guarding or building up our self-esteem. We should never have to worry about ourselves, because others are loving and serving us, even submitting to us with the result that we have every confidence that we are valued and loved. When we in turn submit to others and esteem them, not only are they built up, but we are too. We are built up because in submitting ourselves to others and deferring to them out of love for Christ, we end up being like Jesus. Whenever we live and love like Jesus there is an empowering as well as a blessing that comes our way.

But let me give you an even deeper reason to submit to others. It is not simply in order to be a part of God's plan to feel better about yourself and have your esteem built up. The real reason to submit to others is given in Ephesians 5:21: we do it out of reverence for Christ. So what does that mean? Jesus made a big deal out of saying that whenever we serve the poor, visit the prisoner, comfort the sick, and so on we do these things for Jesus and in fact do them to Him. When you feed a hungry person, you are feeding Jesus. When you clothe a naked person, you are clothing Jesus. When you house a homeless person, you are housing Jesus. Likewise, when you submit to a brother or sister in Christ, you are submitting to Jesus. You submit to Jesus as He lives in them. So out of reverence for Jesus in them, you need to consider them before yourself. You need to honor them instead of yourself.

When we submit in that way, it is not about us putting ourselves down. It is really about lifting them up. When a husband submits to his wife it is in order to help her become the most wonderful person in Christ that she can be. He lifts her up. And in the amazing way that God works, that husband ends up being lifted in the process, too. How? Well, he is one with his wife, so if she is lifted up, so is he. As Paul says, "If one of us is honored, we are all honored" (1 Corinthians 12:26). When a parent submits their own desires for the sake of a child and the child is lifted up in love and esteem, then the parent is too, because they are a part of one another. In the Body of Christ we are all part of one another, and when we lift one another up by submitting to one another, in a miraculous way we are all lifted up.

But the flipside is also true. When one of us is put down, we are all put down. If my wife suffers humiliation, so do I. If my kids suffer, so do I. If my brother in Christ suffers, so do I. So if I try to raise myself up by putting others beneath me, what

I really end up doing is pushing all of us down. By trying to raise myself up I actually lower myself, because I am spiritually tethered to those I am pushing beneath me. I don't even realize that, as a result, we are all sinking. How much better is it to willingly submit myself to the task of raising others higher and being pulled aloft by the upward momentum of my connection to them?

"Wives, submit to your husbands." It used to be those words were heard in nearly every Christian wedding. Today they are hardly ever spoken, and in fact are intentionally avoided. Certainly part of the reason for the change has much to do with a renewed sense of the need for greater equality. But it also has a great deal to do with the fact that over the years these words have been used as a hammer to get women to do whatever a man says, no matter what. The fact is, these words are avoided today by men and women in large part because most people have no clue what Paul was really saying. So here is your chance to finally get a correct understanding of this very provocative portion of Scripture.

In order to understand what Paul meant we absolutely must get the context. That means ignoring the little "helpful" headings that most publishers put throughout the passages of your Bible. The passage in question is Ephesian 5:21-33. Let me reproduce it exactly as it is found in the English Standard Version. Nearly every publisher has done something like this, so I just use this as one example:

²¹*submitting to one another out of reverence for Christ.*

Wives and Husbands

²²*Wives, submit to your own husbands, as to the Lord.* ²³*For the husband is the head of the wife even as Christ is the head of the church, his body, and is himself its Savior.* ²⁴*Now as the church submits to Christ, so also wives should submit in everything to their husbands.*

²⁵Husbands, love your wives, as Christ loved the church and gave himself up for her, ²⁶that he might sanctify her, having cleansed her by the washing of water with the word, ²⁷so that he might present the church to himself in splendor, without spot or wrinkle or any such thing, that she might be holy and without blemish. ²⁸In the same way husbands should love their wives as their own bodies. He who loves his wife loves himself. ²⁹For no one ever hated his own flesh, but nourishes and cherishes it, just as Christ does the church, ³⁰because we are members of his body. ³¹"Therefore a man shall leave his father and mother and hold fast to his wife, and the two shall become one flesh." ³²This mystery is profound, and I am saying that it refers to Christ and the church. ³³However, let each one of you love his wife as himself, and let the wife see that she respects her husband.

Did you notice the helpful header that the publishers inserted between verse 21, which tells us to submit to one another, and verse 22, which tells wives to submit to husbands? In an attempt to be helpful they have placed a nice bold phrase telling us that the next section is about wives and husbands. As helpful as that may be, it also serves to detach the following teaching about relationships from the foundational principle that is to guide them. Paul didn't put a subject header between verses 21 and 22, because they are part of the same subject. We are not to separate the overarching command to submit to one another out of reverence for Christ from the detailed examples that follow telling us what that submission looks like between husbands and wives, parents and children, even between slaves and masters.

Instead of reading this section in its full context what usually happens is that people jump right in on verse 22: "Wives, submit to your husbands." Any discussion of submission starts and stops with the wife submitting to her husband.

So let's take out this little helpful added heading and read verse 21 in context with verses 22-33. Verse 21 is an instruction for all of us to submit to one another out of reverence for Christ. It is only then that we can fully understand how in various life situations we are to submit to one another. Paul says, "Wives, here is what submission to your husband means in your life." But then he immediately goes to the husbands and says, "This is what submission to your wife looks like for you. Love your wife in the same way Christ loves the church. Lay down your life for her."

Yes, wives are to submit to their husbands in the same way the church submits to Christ. What does that look like? It means following his lead and serving him out of love. It is not a blind obedience but a following that comes from a relationship of trust and mutual esteem. Husbands are to submit their desires to their wives by serving them to the point of death. Husbands are to "die to themselves" and do all they can to help their wives become the beautiful, precious bride that Christ also has in mind for the church. For most men the idea of laying down their life for their wife will immediately go to fighting off an attacker or pushing her away from an oncoming bus while taking a grille to the chest. The chances of either of those situations arising are astronomically slim. What is far more likely is that husbands will be asked to die to themselves and submit to their wives by doing the dishes, caring for the kids so she can have a day away, ironing her clothes, or making her lunch. It includes helping her achieve her dreams and become all that God made her to be. It means putting her first.

For wives, submission means putting him first. It means to honor and respect him. I have seen far too many cases of wives who never have an encouraging word for their husband. They never have an honoring or respectful thing to say about him or to him. In fact, in our culture ridiculing a husband has almost become a national sport. How hard is it to find something nice to say about the person to whom you are married? Every man marries a woman wanting her to think that he is the greatest guy in the world. When all he gets is berating and ridicule, the relationship is in deep trouble.

Some will disagree with me that Paul is talking about mutual submission between husbands and wives, and try to make a distinction between a wife's submission to her husband and a husband loving his wife by laying down his life. I say they are both submission. If we define submission only as obeying someone's orders, then no, they are not the same thing. But that is a limited definition of submission that does not fit the biblical concept. In fact, as Clinton Arnold points out in his commentary, *Ephesians (Zondervan Exegetical Commentary on the New Testament)*, the word used in Ephesians 5:21-22 is not the word for "obey." Paul uses the word *hypostasso* in verses 21-22, while in Ephesians 6:1 when telling children to obey parents he uses *hupokouo*. Arnold comments:

> *Although the English term "submit" is viewed in a pejorative way today and is often seen as a sign of weakness or as something one should resist at all costs, it should not be seen in such negative terms here. In general, the verb is widely used for the proper social ordering of people, as, for example, warriors giving their allegiance to their commander ... Paul will elaborate on his expectation that "submission" should characterize the response of the wife to the husband in the divinely ordered marriage roles (Ephesians 5:22-33). His appeal here, however, takes an unexpected twist. He calls for all believers to submit "to one another", not just to those in leadership roles. By expressing himself this way, Paul subverts the normal usage of the term to convey the idea that all believers should defer to one another in the life of the Christian community.*

In other words, this is not about blind obedience to another person. Paul's understanding of submission in a Christian context is about deferring to the needs of others as a Christlike act of service. Wives are to defer to the leadership of their husband for the sake of order in the relationship. This doesn't mean she has no voice, cannot offer ideas or opinions, or even disagree with her husband. What it means is that in the end, when he makes a decision on something, it is in her power to at that time set aside her preference and defer to him.

This works from the other direction as well. When Paul speaks to husbands he calls them to love their wives in the same way Christ loved the church. It is intended to be for the benefit of the wife as Christ's sacrifice was for the benefit of the church. That requires a husband to submit his wants and desires and set them aside for the sake of his wife's benefit. Jesus would have preferred not to go to the cross, as evidenced by His prayer in John 17. But for the sake of the church and out of love for the Father, He set aside His desire and submitted it to the good of others.

Paul takes up this same idea in Philippians 2:3-8:

"Do nothing from selfish ambition or conceit, but in humility count others more significant than yourselves. Let each of you look not only to his own interests, but also to the interests of others. Have this mind among yourselves, which is yours in Christ Jesus, who, though he was in the form of God, did not count equality with God a thing to be grasped, but emptied himself, by taking the form of a servant, being born in the likeness of men. And being found in human form, he humbled himself by becoming obedient to the point of death, even death on a cross."

That is a beautiful description of what submission to one another is supposed to look like. Each follower of Christ is looking out for the needs of others at least as much as they are looking out for their own. In practice it should be more so, just as Jesus looked more to our needs than His own. A husband who puts the needs of his wife above his own will be submitting himself to the benefit of his wife. A wife who honors her husband by following his lead will be submitting herself to her husband for his benefit. I cannot say it enough: This verse is not about blind obedience, submitting to some sort of tyrannical rule in a relationship. It is about mutual respect and submission to a fellow follower of Christ, out of reverence for Christ.

WHEN NOT TO SUBMIT

Shortly after Jesus ascended to heaven, Peter and John were arrested for preaching the name of Jesus and taken before the religious rulers. They were commanded to stop preaching in the name of Jesus and stop trying to convert people to Him. But Peter and John replied: *"But Peter and John answered them, 'Whether it is right in the sight of God to listen to you rather than to God, you must judge, for we cannot but speak of what we have seen and heard'"* (Acts 4:19-20).

The decision was between obeying God or obeying man. Peter and John had received a clear and specific command from Jesus: "Go and preach the gospel to all the world." The religious leaders gave them a clear and specific command to not preach. The choice was obvious; they had to obey God rather than man. So they continued to preach. The result was that they were arrested and beaten and the apostle James was executed.

A similar event took place in the Old Testament. The prophet Daniel was forbidden to pray to anyone except King Darius. God had made it clear that only He was to be the object of our prayer life, and that we should never pray to a false god. Daniel had no choice but to continue to pray as he had always done. As a result he was arrested and thrown into a lion's den. God in His mercy rescued Daniel from the lions.

In both cases there was a clear command from God about what to do. When those in authority tried to require God's people to violate His command, the only choice was to rebel against the human authority and obey God. There was no option of deferring to the other for his or her benefit, since violating a clear command from God benefits no one. But it must not be forgotten that refusing to obey the human authority and follow God does not come with a guarantee that you will not suffer for your rebellion. Daniel was thrown to the lions and God saved him, but James was beheaded for insisting on preaching the name of Jesus. We make a grave mistake when we think that obeying God rather than men should result in things being wonderful for us. Often that is not the case. If your boss wants you to do something illegal or unethical and you rightly refuse, he may still fire you. In that case the Bible would actually have us rejoice in the blessing of suffering for doing good:

"For what credit is it if, when you sin and are beaten for it, you endure? But if when you do good and suffer for it you endure, this is a gracious thing in the sight of God" (1 Peter 2:20).

CHAPTER 20

DO NOT BE UNEQUALLY YOKED

"Do not be unequally yoked with unbelievers. For what partnership has righteousness with lawlessness? Or what fellowship has light with darkness?"
— 2 Corinthians 6:14

IN RECENT WEEKS I have had several people quote this verse to me. They have done so in an attempt to explain why Christians should never be a partner with or cooperate with people who are not Christians. In the context of the discussions it is clear that they are talking about not partnering with non-Christians on any level. Is that really what Paul intends? Are we to not have any dealings of cooperation or partnership with people who do not share our faith in Christ?

If Paul meant that we are to have no association or dealings with unbelievers, then I have found my first-ever, clear example of the Bible being in contradiction with itself. In fact, it would mean that Paul is in contradiction with himself in his communication to these same Christians in Corinth. In his first letter to the Corinthians Paul says that he never intended for them to have no association with "sinners," since to accomplish that they would have to leave the world. Paul actually pushes in the opposite direction: we are to be engaged with the lost people of the world so that they come to know Christ. We are ambassadors for Christ. We are witnesses to Jesus. We cannot do that if we don't engage others in some kind of relationship. So the question is, What kinds of relationships are legitimate between followers of Jesus and those who are not, and what kinds of relationships are forbidden?

The New American Standard Bible translation quoted above says that we are not to be unequally bound together with unbelievers. The King James Version says, "Do not be unequally yoked." The words are reminiscent of Deuteronomy 22:10, which instructs God's people not to yoke together a oxen and a donkey in the same team pulling a plow. The two would be mismatched and result in disaster. Being yoked together is a particular kind of relationship. It is one of being bound together. It is one that you cannot easily extricate yourself from. Another good word of translation for yoked would be "mismatched."

The most common understanding of 2 Corinthians 6:14 is that Paul is telling Christians not to marry unbelievers. He clearly said this in his first letter to the Corinthians. That is an appropriate interpretation and application. Contrary to the wisdom of our age that says what we believe is really not important in the grand scheme of things, and that two different religions should have no problem living under the same roof, the reality is the opposite. If you are a follower of Jesus Christ you have no business entering into a marriage with a non-Christian. For starters, that which is most important in your life, or at least should be—your relationship with Christ—is not important to that potential spouse. You are starting off like that oxen and donkey trying to plow a field together. It just doesn't work. More than that, as a follower of Christ you are united with Christ and He dwells in you by the presence of the Holy Spirit. With your spouse you are also to become one. You are to be united in a deep and very real spiritual way. That can't happen if your spirit is united with Christ and theirs is not.

But the imagery and context here goes beyond that of marriage. The verses following 6:14 bring to mind images related to worship. The Corinthians had a huge problem, living in the midst of numerous temples to false gods and a society that was built on such idolatry. Paul was telling the Corinthians to make sure that they kept their fellowship with Christ and their worship of God free from the pollution of idolatry. The references to the Temple, to idols, to Belial, and a quote from Leviticus and Isaiah bring the worship context to the foreground. This is a verse about compromising who God is and our worship of Him. We are not to mix our religious practices with the idolatry of the world.

That does not mean that we can't be a business partner with a non-Christian. We certainly need to be wise about the dangers that can result in having two different worldviews. But it does not mean that you can't have a business contract with a non-Christian. It doesn't mean that you can't cooperate with a non-Christian for a common cause. If a Muslim and a Christian and an atheist all want to end abortion, then there is no reason not to work together. They may have different reasons for wanting the same result but that is no reason not to find common ground for common good.

We need to be very careful in declaring that we are not to engage with, and work with, those who do not follow Christ. The danger is that we will draw into our own little Christian ghetto more and more. We cannot be salt if we are not in contact with the world. We cannot be light if we are hidden under a basket. The answer is not withdrawal. The answer is wise engagement under the influence of the Holy Spirit and guidance of God's Word. We need to know where the line is and be sure not to cross it. That line would be whenever we are so "yoked" together that we are bound and unable to extricate ourselves, or when the involvement clearly endorses the worship of false gods. With those two safeguards we are to be ambassadors who engage the world for Jesus' sake.

[HAPTER 21

JUDGE NOT

" 'Judge not, that you be not judged. For with the judgment you pronounce you will be judged, and with the measure you use it will be measured to you. Why do you see the speck that is in your brother's eye, but do not notice the log that is in your own eye? Or how can you say to your brother, "Let me take the speck out of your eye," when there is the log in your own eye? You hypocrite, first take the log out of your own eye, and then you will see clearly to take the speck out of your brother's eye.' " — Matthew 7:1-5

" 'Do not judge by appearances, but judge with right judgment.' " — John 7:24

IT MAY BE THE MOST often-quoted and yet most misunderstood verse in the whole Bible. People who have never even cracked open a Bible have heard and quoted Matthew 7:1: "Do not judge so that you will not be judged."

Usually that verse is used like a hammer to immediately stop any discussion about the rightness or wrongness of a person's behavior. Almost invariably when someone claims that a certain action or behavior is wrong, someone else will say, "But Jesus said we are not to judge anyone." The clear implication is that we can never say if some behavior is sin or not because we are not to judge. Sometimes these words are shouted out in anger and rage: "You can't judge me!"

What is possibly more amazing than the fact that so many people quote this verse and the concept of not judging, is that so many people could get the real meaning so completely wrong. This is especially true since the context makes it clear what Jesus meant by these words. When Jesus said that we should not judge unless we be judged also, He was not saying that we are to never judge if behavior is sin or not. What He was doing was giving us a caution to make sure that we are willing to be judged by the same standard of judgment. This verse is not a warning against judging an action. It is a warning against self-deception and hypocrisy.

The way we know this is the same way that we usually know what the Bible teaches. We look at the context. The verse that immediately follows helps explain what Jesus was saying. Matthew 7:2 goes on: "For in the way you judge, you will be judged; and by your standard of measure, it will be measured to you." In other words, if you are going to say that what someone else is doing is wrong, then you better be prepared to be judged by the same standard. If you don't want your life to be scrutinized, then don't judge others. If you can stand the scrutiny, then go ahead. Think of Al Gore telling us that we need to cut down our energy use in order to save the planet and then finding out that he has three large homes and the carbon footprint of Godzilla. He needed to read this verse first.

Just in case we still have not figured out that this is not a complete prohibition on judging behavior, the next few verses make it even more clear:

"Why do you look at the speck that is in your brother's eye, but do not notice the log that is in your own eye? Or how can you say to your brother, 'Let me take the speck out of your eye,' and behold, the log is in your own eye? You hypocrite, first take the log out of your own eye, and then you will see clearly to take the speck out of your brother's eye" (Matthew 7:3-5).

Before you ever start to tell someone else what is wrong with their life, make sure you take a good look at your own life first. But notice, Jesus does not say, "Take the log out of your own eye and don't say anything about the speck in the other person's eye." That would be the result of never judging anyone about anything. Instead, Jesus says that after you take care of your own stuff, then go and help your brother. So you are to help them with their issue, but only once you have done a personal spiritual check to make sure that you are right with God.

We need to see this as a matter of helping someone, not beating them down. Jesus used the example of having something in your eye. In order to get it out, often you need the help of someone else to see it and remove it. When we see something wrong in the life of a friend we need to point it out and help them deal with it. When we do that, we are serving them not condemning them. What this is really all about is determining if something is right or wrong behavior, sin or not sin. We can and should do that with a loving attitude and not a condemning, superior, hypocritical attitude. Pointing out destructive behavior in another person is actually an incredible and brave way to love your neighbor. We understand this when the situation becomes so serious as to require an intervention. How much more loving would it be to step in long before it got so serious?

There are a couple of final reasons why this verse cannot mean that we are never to judge if what a person does is right or wrong. First, Jesus makes it very clear that we are to forgive people when they sin against us. In the Lord's Prayer we pray that God would forgive us as we forgive others. Well, in order to forgive someone you have to first "judge" that they have done something wrong. The very act of forgiveness that Jesus teaches so clearly requires that we identify some behavior as wrong. To fail to judge it as wrong or sinful in the first place makes it impossible to forgive.

Second, the Bible is filled with admonitions that we avoid evil, flee from temptation, and cling to what is good and lovely. In order to do that, we have to make judgment calls. We have to decide that one thing is good and another is not. We make these decisions all the time as a matter of course. We do it if we are a follower of Jesus or not. Everyone has some things that they decide are right to do and others that are not. Every society and culture has these things, and every member of those cultures has to think and decide, has to judge what behaviors fit the standard.

Bursting forth with the words "Judge not" should in no way intimidate anyone from deciding if something is sinful or not. If anything slows us in judging it should be the warning from Jesus that we not be hypocrites who are unable or unwilling to live according to that same standard.

CHAPTER 22

TREAT THEM LIKE AN UNBELIEVER

" 'If your brother sins against you, go and tell him his fault, between you and him alone. If he listens to you, you have gained your brother. But if he does not listen, take one or two others along with you, that every charge may be established by the evidence of two or three witnesses. If he refuses to listen to them, tell it to the church. And if he refuses to listen even to the church, let him be to you as a Gentile and a tax collector.' " — Matthew 18:15-17

"It is actually reported that there is sexual immorality among you, and of a kind that is not tolerated even among pagans, for a man has his father's wife. And you are arrogant! Ought you not rather to mourn? Let him who has done this be removed from among you." — 1 Corinthians 5:1-2

THERE IS A HISTORY in much of the church that calls for shunning people who do not repent of sin. In part that practice is picked up from the words of Jesus in Matthew 18, where He says that if a person refuses to repent after a process that has involved three different encounters calling for them to repent, then they should be "treated like a pagan or tax collector."

From that passage, as well as numerous other places in the New Testament, it is apparent that Christians must be concerned about the behavior of people within the body we call the church. Although Christians are to be loving and welcoming to people from every and any place in life, there is still an expected level of behavior that should be exhibited by someone who claims to be a Christ-follower.

When Jesus teaches about reconciliation in Matthew 18—for that is what the passage is all about—He gives instructions on how to deal with someone who has wronged you, who has sinned against you. The three-step process is intended to restore the relationship. It is assumed that the relationship has already suffered when He speaks of a person who has sinned against you. That action—be it stealing from you, slandering your name, physically or verbally assaulting you, or any other sinful behavior—has broken the relationship to some degree. As followers of Christ we are to be united to one another, as the Son and Father are united to each other (John 17). So when a relationship is broken we must work hard to restore it if for no other reason than disunity in the Body of Christ is a dishonor to the name of Christ we claim.

We see the importance of unity in the church when we hear the reactions of those outside it. Non-Christians can readily use the divisiveness and backbiting that is evident in the church as an understandable reason to stay away from church and, more importantly, from Jesus. The refrain is repeated often: "If that is how Christians treat one another, then I don't want any part of it."

Therefore one important reason to deal with sinful behavior in the church is so that there is a level of behavior that is honoring to Christ and attractive to people who are not following Him. This is true not only when it comes to internal divisions between followers of Christ but also when it comes to other types of moral and ethical behavior. When huge numbers of people think the church is full of hypocrites we have a serious public image problem. Christians who claim to love their neighbor and then treat them like dirt are not helping the cause of Christ. Some level of church discipline is needed to protect the integrity of Christ and the ministry of the church.

This should not even be something that is up for debate. In the secular world it is expected that people have certain levels of behavior in order to be part of an organization. Most companies have standards of conduct, some of which get as specific as dress codes and behavior when you are not on the clock. Even professional sports teams will have contract clauses that relate to conduct detrimental to the team or the league. People have no problem with these things and seem to even think they are important and beneficial. Well, if the off-the-field behavior of a professional football player can be detrimental to the team, resulting in suspension or even termination, how much more important is the 24/7 behavior of a Christ-follower? What eternal damage is done when we claim the name of Christ and live contrary to the most basic of His commands?

There will, of course, be times when people within the church refuse to acknowledge they have done wrong. Even after repeated attempts like the three-step process outlined by Jesus, some people will not budge. They will not admit any wrongdoing, and refuse to take the steps needed to repent or restore unity. It is at that point that Jesus says to treat them like a pagan or a tax collector.

So just what does that mean? Jesus gives us the answer, and it is far different from the shunning, rejection, and self-righteous attitude that are so often practiced by Christians. To understand what Jesus means to treat someone as a pagan and a tax collector we only need to look at how Jesus treated them. For that we have abundant examples in the New Testament.

When we see Jesus engaging pagans and tax collectors, or any other group of unbelieving sinners, we see someone who gives them huge amounts of time, attention, and grace. So much so that the religious leaders accuse Him of being one of those pagans! In Matthew 11:19, Jesus says that they accuse Him of being a drunkard because He spends so much time with the sinners. Spending any time with such people was taboo for the religious leaders of Jesus' day. They were convinced that if they got near such people, especially in as intimate a setting as a meal in a pagan's home, that they would somehow become spiritually defiled. They avoided pagans at all costs. Tax collectors were in the same category because of their reputation as thieves, and for their participation with the occupying Roman army in collecting taxes. They were both sinners and traitors. They were so looked down upon that Pharisees, the religious legalists of the day, would regularly pray and thank God that they did not have to suffer the indignity of being a tax collector.

Far different from the religious elite, Jesus showed unending love and respect to these "pagans and tax-collectors." He treated them with the dignity that was due someone created in the image of God. He didn't ignore their sin, and He certainly did not condone it. He readily admitted that they were sinners, but also called them to a higher moral standard. When a woman who was caught in adultery was brought to Jesus He forgave her and said, "Go and sin no more" (John 8:11). He acknowledged that what she did was wrong, but He also gave her mercy and grace. That was His pattern. He gave people grace and mercy and treated them with dignity, while calling them to a more holy way of life.

It must be noted that Jesus spent a great deal of time with such people. In fact He would go out of His way to do so. The woman at the well, the home of Zacchaeus the tax-collector, and the wedding at Cana are all examples of Jesus making time to spend with people who were not perfect, cleaned-up, respectable church-going types. What He did was love them. He loved them by being with them. He reached out to them where they were but at the same time made it clear there they needed to abandon where they were and how they were living and give themselves completely to God by following Him.

But, you may ask, aren't we supposed to love everyone? If so, in what way is our treatment of someone who is a tax collector or pagan different from how we treat a brother or sister in Christ? Because clearly, from what Jesus says in Matthew 18, there is a difference. If a brother or sister in Christ will not repent and will not be reconciled then we are to start treating them like a pagan and a tax collector. So what is the difference in our treatment of them if we are supposed to love everyone? That is the heart of the issue. This is about how you treat a person who is also a follower of Christ who will not be reconciled to you. That person you are to treat like a pagan or tax collector. So we love them. That is obvious and makes sense. But in what way is it different?

What do you not do with people outside the Body of Christ that you do with people inside? What is different? One thing is you do not have communion with them. Communion, the Lord's Supper, is to be a believer-only event. In the early church it was a meal, just like the Last Supper in the upper room. It was an intimate religious and social event that included a confession of faith in Jesus as Lord, looking forward to His return. Only followers of Christ participated in it. In fact, as worship services became more public and had non-believers present, when it came time for communion the non-believers would be dismissed. It is from this biblical concept that the Roman Catholic Church denies communion to people who are not in good standing. It is a practice that most Protestant churches also have in their history, though in recent decades that has faded almost to the point of being non-existent. So what is being said is that treating someone like a pagan or tax collector means that you do not include him or her in things that are reserved for followers of Jesus. You don't have communion with them. You don't marry them. You probably don't pray with them, in the sense of having a prayer time in which they are an equal participant—though you can and should pray for them. You would not allow them to serve in a position of spiritual leadership, but you would allow them to serve in some capacity that does not require faith in Christ. I have had non-believers go on mission trips that did not require faith in Christ, only the ability to swing a hammer. They were not expected to share the gospel with someone. They didn't know the gospel. But they knew construction and could serve in that capacity while followers of Christ served along with them and shared the gospel.

In a real-life, first-century situation the Apostle Paul had to deal with a serious moral breach that was occurring in the church in Corinth. The situation that arose involved a man who was sleeping with his father's wife. The best explanation is that this was his stepmother, not his biological mother. To make matters worse, it appears that some were claiming that since they now had freedom in Christ and were not under the law, this was acceptable behavior. Paul was forced to vehemently point out how wrong their thinking was on this, and that even pagans knew that you didn't have sex with your father's wife!

Paul urged the church to call the brother concerned to repentance for the sake of obedience to Christ and also because of not wanting the watching pagan world to get the wrong idea about Christians. The church did confront the man but he initially refused to repent. Paul's words were strong at this point, urging the church to not associate with such a man. In typical Christian fashion they had understood not to associate with such sinners to mean avoiding pagans at all costs. Paul clarified that and said, "No, I am speaking of a brother in Christ, not the pagan outside Christ." Eventually the young man did repent, but once again the church got it wrong. They refused to allow him back into the fellowship, so Paul once again had to write to them and this time urge them to receive the man back into the fellowship since that was the whole point of the discipline. It was exactly in line with what Jesus previously said in Matthew 18.

All of that is well and good, but there is a dilemma. On the face of it Paul's words about how to treat the unrepentant man seem to be far more strict and harsh than those of Jesus. It is here that people go to support the idea of a total shunning of the brother or sister who will not repent. In particular Paul says this: *"But now I am writing to you not to associate with anyone who bears the name of brother if he is guilty of sexual immorality or greed, or is an idolater, reviler, drunkard, or swindler—not even to eat with such a one"* (1 Corinthians 5:11).

That seems to be very clear and very direct: Do not even associate with such a brother, don't even share a meal with him. This is especially puzzling since in his letters to the Christians in Corinth Paul told them that if they could handle it they could eat a meal in the home of a pagan, even if the food had been offered as a sacrifice to an idol or a false god. The treatment of an unrepentant brother seems extreme by comparison. Where was the grace, mercy, forgiveness, and love that should characterize Christian behavior towards others?

What we need to understand is the damage that is done to the cause of Christ when followers behave badly. Excommunication—for that is what we are talking about here—is the only effective way to demonstrate both to the church and to the world that there is an expected standard of moral and ethical behavior that Christ-followers should exhibit. Since we should expect better behavior from Christians it stands to reason that the repercussions for falling short are more severe than what pagans and tax collectors would experience.

This is a principle that shows up in James 3:1: *"Not many of you should become teachers, my brothers, for you know that we who teach will be judged with greater strictness."* The point here is in line with Jesus' statement that to whom much is given is much required. If one is given the privilege of teaching the things of

God, then one's behavior in relation to that teaching should be greater than the average Christ-follower. Failure for it to be so will result in greater scrutiny on the Day of Judgment. Likewise a typical Christ-follower who has been given so much more in the way of salvation and a relationship with Christ should behave in a way that is ethically and morally more pure than your average pagan or tax collector. Failure to do so would understandably result in more serious consequences.

Again, it needs to be said that this excommunication is not vindictive but redemptive. Paul always kept the goal in front of the Corinthians, as Jesus did in Matthew 18. It was to restore the brother to fellowship. There should never be any anger towards them. There should never be a total rejection of them. There should never be any of the complete "shunning" that has been church practice in the past. Such actions serve only to drive those disciplined further away in despair. They still need to know that they are loved and will be welcomed back into the fellowship and full communion upon repentance.

When Paul says to not even associate with such a person we need to understand what he is saying in a first-century context. In the twenty-first century we use words about relationships in a far more loose and casual way than they would have then. Take "friend." How many Facebook "friends" do you have? How many of them have you never met face to face? When we talk about fellowship today it usually brings to mind a time between church services where there is coffee and donuts. Not so for the first-century believers. For them words of relationship were far more meaningful than for most people today. It was incredibly significant when Jesus said in John 15:15: *"No longer do I call you servants, for the servant does not know what his master is doing; but I have called you friends, for all that I have heard from my Father I have made known to you."*

He had been with the disciples nearly day and night for three years, and finally called them friends. That was a huge step. In a similar way fellowship—*koinonia* in the Greek—is not just standing around between services, hiding behind a cup of coffee while exchanging pleasantries. Biblical fellowship is "shared life." There is an intimacy associated with it that is often accompanied by a meal. Eating together was an intimate thing in the first century, as it is today in many cultures. You would often eat out of common bowls and you used your hands.

The point of all this is that when Paul says do not even associate with such a one, he is not saying, "Don't talk to them, don't say hello to them, don't even give them a head nod of recognition." What he is saying is that you cannot have the kind of intermingling—for that is what the word "associate" means in the original—that you must have for real fellowship and communion. This is especially true when it comes to the Lord's Supper, communion, which was not just a wafer and a miniature shot glass with juice in it. Communion was a full-on meal like the Passover. It was reserved for followers of Christ. The unrepentant brother had to be excluded, excommunicated, from that association for his own good and the good of Christ.

The point is there are lots of things that you can and should do with tax collectors and pagans if you want to be like Jesus. Likewise there are lots of things that you can and should do with the brother or sister in Christ who has sinned against you. There are activities in which the unrepentant brother or sister must not be included. The goal of all of this for either group is to see demonstrated the love, grace, and mercy of God in order to lead them to repentance and restored relationships with you and Jesus. Paul said in Romans 2:4 that it is God's kindness that leads us to repentance. That kindness should be evident in our dealings with one another, even if we are required to treat someone as a tax collector or sinner. The goal of such treatment is not to exclude them from the fellowship of the Body, but to lead them back to it in a way that brings glory to God. You can't do that if you never demonstrate love towards them as you would to anyone who needs to come to Christ.

CHAPTER 23

YOU ARE THE LIGHT OF THE WORLD

" 'You are the light of the world. A city set on a hill cannot be hidden. Nor do people light a lamp and put it under a basket, but on a stand, and it gives light to all in the house.' " — Matthew 5:14-15

"Again Jesus spoke to them, saying, 'I am the light of the world. Whoever follows me will not walk in darkness, but will have the light of life.' " — John 8:12

THOROUGHLY ENJOYED THE years I served as a youth pastor. It was an awesome time! I would pick out stuff that I loved to do and that became the stuff that the youth group did; it's one of the perks of being a youth pastor. Numerous trips to Tennessee to go hiking, camping, and rock climbing, whitewater rafting on Ohiopyle in western Pennsylvania, weekend retreats in the Appalachian Mountains, and mission trips to Mexico were all part of my youth ministry agenda.

Perhaps one of the most unique things we did was caving. There is nothing quite like getting a group of teenagers underground with helmets and flashlights and poking around through cracks and crevices, crawling on your belly through the mud with the ceiling only inches above you. The sense of adventure was high and there were quite a few folks who had to face some fears of tight places and darkness.

Standard operating procedure was to get everyone together in one place at some point, usually as large a "room" as we could find, and turn off all the flashlights. You don't know darkness until you are a few hundred feet underground and the lights go out. No matter how long you sit in the dark your eyes never adjust. There isn't the slightest bit of light for them to latch onto. It is dark, dark, dark. In that darkness the slightest pinpoint of light takes on a whole new power. It becomes a beacon of hope, a way of escape, a symbol of life. It draws you, calls you, reaches out to you, and warms your soul.

When Jesus told His disciples that they were the light of the world, a city set on a hill, they understood perfectly what He meant by those words. They, and by association all Christ-followers throughout history, are a beacon of hope, a way of escape, a symbol of life. That is because at night the light coming from a distant city, most often set on a hilltop, meant that protection and rest were within reach.

Until Edison invented the light bulb and electric power plants started supplying light to cities, darkness was the norm once the sun went down. There would obviously be some light from fires that people used to warm themselves, or from small oil lanterns, but it was nothing like today. The view from space at night in the first century would have shown a dark planet. The light from campfires and oil lamps would have been too small to see. The view from space at night in the twenty-first century gives you a detailed picture of where people live. All of Europe, both American seaboards, and huge patches of massive cities on every continent—with the exception of Antarctica—would be glowing brilliantly from the lights shining from buildings, highways, sports stadiums, and more.

Several years ago I was with a group of folks from Northland Church as we traveled to the tiny nation of Swaziland in southern Africa. We joined up with a group of South African Christians to spend ten days serving at a school for AIDS orphans and other vulnerable children. Upon flying into Johannesburg and meeting the South Africans we took a bus to "Swazi." What should have been a six-hour trip took eleven. As a result we arrived well past midnight. It was a clear night, and I knew we were well out into the boonies because the little bit of light we saw along the way was mostly from small, individual huts off in the distance. Our destination was a game park that had no electricity. As we stepped off the bus I looked up into that clear, dark sky and stood in awe and wonder. Because there was little to no ambient light to drown out the stars, what I saw looked as if someone had splashed a cosmic-sized glass of milk across the heavens. For the first time in my life I truly understood what was meant by the name, the Milky Way. I must have stood there for five minutes just looking up. Once I finally got moving I found myself constantly stopping and gazing skyward. It was breathtaking.

Those stars stood out as they did because there was only darkness otherwise. The contrast between the light and the dark was stunning. I was drawn to the light of those stars just as ancient travelers were drawn to the light of a city set on a hill. Jesus says that His followers should shine in that same way. Our lives should be such that people living in darkness see that light and are drawn to it, inspired by it, and filled with hope and awe and wonder by it. That is what Jesus wants and expects from His followers when He speaks of being the light of the world. He wants people to come to a relationship with Him because of what they see in His followers.

There is a much-misused quote from Francis of Assisi that says, "Preach the Gospel at all times. When necessary use words." The misuse of this quote is the idea that we should speak as little as possible when it comes to sharing the gospel, that actions are enough. Scripture is adamant that we need to speak the gospel as well as live it. Paul tells Timothy that he must preach the gospel both in season and out of season (2 Timothy 4:2). He also tells the church in Rome that it is not possible for people to come to faith in Christ unless the gospel is preached:

"How then will they call on him in whom they have not believed? And how are they to believe in him of whom they have never heard? And how are they to hear without someone preaching?" (Romans 10:14)

The way we should understand the words of Francis is that both our good works and our good words are necessary for people to come to faith in Christ. At all times our lives' good works should be evident. There will be times when it is necessary to then explain the basis of our good works so that people can be pointed to Jesus. What we don't want is for people to think that we are just nice folks, and get the praise and credit for our mercy, compassion, and love of neighbor. Immediately following His words telling us that we are the light of the world Jesus gives the reason for our light to shine:

"In the same way, let your light shine before others, so that they may see your good works and give glory to your Father who is in heaven" (Matthew 5:16).

When we speak about being provocative this is exactly what is meant. When you exhibit love towards others by serving them it is going to provoke a response. People will often comment on your kindness, and maybe even ask why you are doing what you are doing. It is at that point that we are given the freedom to point to Jesus as the reason for our love and kindness, not anything in us.

What is truly provocative from the perspective of what God has said is that Jesus is giving us the responsibility and opportunity to point a lost and dying world in the direction of life and light. We are the light of the world. We are what people can see that is supposed to give them hope and point them to Jesus who is the ultimate light of the world:

"Again Jesus spoke to them, saying, 'I am the light of the world. Whoever follows me will not walk in darkness, but will have the light of life'" (John 8:12).

There is an identification that Jesus is making between Himself and His followers. He says that He is the light of the world and yet also says that His followers are the light of the world. It really takes us all the way back to the first chapter, where we talked about being made in the image of God. We saw that to be an image-bearer means to represent the original and to in some way stand in for the original on its behalf. When God created the world and made us in His image it was with the intent that we would be the stewards and caretakers of His creation, and that we would act with and under His authority. By saying that He and we are the light of the world, Jesus is reinforcing the role we play as image-bearers.

It is hard to fathom what God was thinking by making us image-bearers at the dawn of creation. We certainly messed that up in a royal way. It is even more mind-boggling to me that, after all the ways in which we turn from Him and against Him, He still wants us to represent Him to the world. I have to wonder if there isn't a better more reliable way for God to be made known to the world. Seriously God, isn't there a plan B that would work better to give you the glory you deserve and have people turn to you? Apparently there isn't. For whatever reason, God continues to give us that responsibility and privilege.

Paul speaks of this when he writes to the Corinthians:

"Therefore, if anyone is in Christ, he is a new creation. The old has passed away; behold, the new has come. All this is from God, who through Christ reconciled us to himself and gave us the ministry of reconciliation; that is, in Christ God was reconciling the world to himself, not counting their trespasses against them, and entrusting to us the message of reconciliation. Therefore, we are ambassadors for Christ, God making his appeal through us. We implore you on behalf of

Christ, be reconciled to God" (2 Corinthians 5:17-20).

An ambassador is in many respects an image-bearer. An ambassador represents and speaks on behalf of and with the authority of the king. When you hear the ambassador, you hear the king. Likewise the ambassador is the embodiment of the people from the realm he or she represents. You gain an impression and understanding of the people from that realm by way of your contact with the ambassador. If the ambassador is a kind and gentle person you will project that onto the other people of that realm and decide that they must also be kind and gentle. If the ambassador is arrogant, judgmental, and hypocritical, you will naturally project all of that onto the people of that realm and decide that they must also be arrogant, judgmental, and hypocritical. It is what we do to try to make sense of the world and give us categories of understanding.

Jesus was well aware of that when He called us to be the light of the world and represent Him. It is why living a Christ-like life is so crucial for anyone who claims to be a Christian. It is why the idea of excommunication that we saw in the previous chapter is so important. If an ambassador is causing havoc in a country by breaking laws, being critically judgmental about the habits and customs of the nation to which they are an ambassador, then the government back home will have no choice but to recall them in disgrace. They cannot be allowed to continue to besmirch the name of their king and country.

On the other hand, when an ambassador does their job well and represents the king with honor, then the people of the land to which they have been sent will welcome them. They will want to know more about their country. Some may even want to leave their homeland and become citizens of the ambassador's land. That is what Paul is talking about when he says we have been given the ministry of reconciliation. God has called us to be the people who point others to Jesus and seek to bring about a reunion, a reconciliation, so that people can go from living in darkness to living in the light of Christ and enjoying heaven for all eternity!

And make no mistake. Spiritually speaking, the world is living in the same darkness as those caves where I had the teenagers turn off their flashlights. The only difference is people don't know they are living in spiritual darkness. They are like the blind salamanders that live in the caves. They have only been in darkness, and so they don't have any idea that it's dark and they are blind. On a certain level those salamanders function just fine. They have learned how to function without light. They eat, they mate, they sleep, and move about. But they are still blind and they still live in darkness.

Jesus said:

"And Jesus came and said to them, 'All authority in heaven and on earth has been given to me. Go therefore and make disciples of all nations, baptizing them in the name of the Father and of the Son and of the Holy Spirit, teaching them to observe all that I have commanded you. And behold, I am with you always, to the end of the age'" (Matthew 28:18-20).

That is the role we have as image-bearers, as the light of the world, as ambassadors for Christ. We have been granted the authority of the King to go into the world with His power and His message so that people would come to know, love, follow, and trust Him. What a provocative God we have! If that call to change the world, to be His light, to bring life and hope and joy and peace, does not provoke some response in you, please, check your pulse.

ABOUT THE AUTHOR

Dan Lacich serves as a pastor at Northland, a Church Distributed, in Longwood, Florida, where he teaches and helps lead the church's effort to train pastors around the world to plant multiplying churches. He has served as Adjunct Faculty at Belhaven University in Orlando, teaching Bible and theology as well as at International Leadership University in the School of Missiology in Burundi, Africa, and is a founding board member of the Global Alliance for Church Multiplication. He and his wife Barbara have been married for 35 years and have three sons, Zachariah, Justin and Garrett.

Blog
www.provocativechristian.com

Email
provocativechristian@gmail.com

Twitter
@dlacich

Mailing Address
Northland Church
530 Dog Track Road
Longwood, FL 32750